COMMERCIAL TO RESIDENTIAL CONVERSIONS

The essential manual for property developers

Commercial to Residential Conversions: The essential manual for property developers

Research by Mark Stokes
Cover Design by Avnie Shah
Email: mark.stokes@equagroup.co.uk
Instagram: markstokes.stokes
Facebook: markstokes.stokes
LinkedIn: mark-stokes
Twitter: @markelstead
www.equagroup.co.uk
www.markstokesuk.com

Disclaimer

Although the author and publisher have made every effort to ensure that the information in this book was correct at the time of printing, the author and publisher do not assume and hereby disclaim any liability to any party for any loss, damage or disruption cause by errors or omissions, whether such errors or omissions result from negligence, accident, or any other cause.

Contents

DEDICATION

I would like to dedicate this book to my wife, Sharon, for her wonderful support, love, companionship and energy, as well as to my four children: Ben, Jack, Katy and Emily who make me so proud and are my constant, my reason 'why' and who I firmly believe have the potential to make a positive change in the world and achieve great things.

This is the poem I read to my wife on our wedding day in 1998 - which means just as much now as it did back then.

THE LIFE THAT I HAVE

The life that I have
Is all that I have
And the life that I have
Is yours.
The love that I have
Of the life that I have
Is yours and yours and yours.
A sleep I shall have
A rest I shall have
Yet death will be but a pause.
For the peace of my years
In the long green grass
Will be yours and yours and yours.

LEO MARKS

My deepest love to you all.
xxxx

ACKNOWLEDGMENTS

There are many people who have had a profound effect and impact on my life, some remain great friends, others I have met briefly on my journey of life and other sadly no longer with us today.

I would like to thank my family for their strong support, guidance and love and who have spurred me on to write this book and achieve the best I can in life. Thanks to Sharon, Ben, Jack, Katy and Emily.

Also to my parents Rachel and Richard for their strong values, principles and enthusiasm which set me on my path for which I will forever be grateful.

To my business partners in our Equa businesses, Nigel Greene, Mike Tivey and Phil Burr - we have seen a lot over the past two decades and experienced many of the highest highs and had challenging times. Your ever-present companionship, drive, counsel and wisdom has been infectious and a continuing source of inspiration to me.

To Avnie Shah for her wonderful support, counsel and amazing work in designing the book cover. Your patience and insightful questions were a revelation in helping create truly professional artwork.

Thanks to Andy McInnes for his wealth of knowledge and inspiration in journalism and publishing.

A big thank you to Naz Stewart and the team at Book Printing UK whose patience, expertise and wisdom has been invaluable.

And finally and with a heavy heart, I remember my great friend Pete Abbott who is sadly no longer with us. Pete had so many rare qualities and was an incredible guy, a wonderful friend and someone who could light up even the darkest day. The world lost an amazing talent and loving human being when you left us Pete, you remain an inspiration and your legacy will not be forgotten.

SECTION ONE
MAKING A START

Does it make my car go faster? - Frank Williams

FOREWORD

My fingers were numb to the bone, my face felt like a block of ice and my leg muscles were beyond aching, twitching involuntarily, blood blisters on both feet and three toenails missing and deep gashes across my shins.

I had been running for 23 ½ hours solid, only to stop to take on food and water at checkpoints. The start line, some 105 miles ago, felt like an eternity ago and my peripheral vision had been reduced to the few meters ahead illuminated under my head torch.

I was in auto pilot, my body and mind conditioned in a plateau of endurance through many hundreds of training hours on lonely trail paths.

And yet in the still freezing early morning darkness my senses felt alert as ever, navigating every bend and junction to avoid errors. The tiredness, bone marrow deep, was gnawing at my soul but the elusive finishing line was only two miles away. In that serene yet excruciating last effort I reached the end of the road, totally spent, utterly content and quietly contemplating achieving my goal. 107 miles in 24 hours non-stop.

There is no pain at the finishing line but what there is the powerful re-emergence of the knowledge that "we are only competing with what we are capable of."

An ultra-endurance marathon will tear you up and spit you out if you are not prepared, both in body and mind - but mostly in mind.

The elite athletes are racing for the best times and places, pitting themselves against each other in a long-haul battle that drags them to the depths of their capabilities and pinnacle of their profession.

For ultra-trail runners like myself, however, we push ourselves to define the depth of our reserve tank, to experience what it takes to achieve and experience the greatest breadth and depth of success our soul can achieve.

Anything is achievable if your attitude, approach and courage is set to grasp the journey with all its twists and turns and to experience a part of life that most choose not to access.

The life of an entrepreneur has its unique blend of opportunity and challenge, of freedom and navigation, of evolution and a continuous quest for creating shared value.

"creating massive shared value, huge return on time invested and enabling impactful change at a societal level"

26 years of corporate life from Engineer to Chairman, Trouble Shooter to Non-Executive Director, Start-up co-founder to Managing Director across four continents has bestowed on me a wealth of life experiences I am extremely grateful for. I have had the opportunity and privilege to work alongside some of the most gifted business minds the world has to offer.

And yet something was missing: A yearning to be in control of my own personal economy – time, wealth in all its forms and security for my family. The freedom to define my own path.

I had been successful in my business life, seized every opportunity and had thrown myself into every situation available – starting companies, closing them, trouble-shooting massive corporate issues, acquisitions and global travel.

There was no destitution, debt or bottom of the barrel brink of life event that triggered my retirement from my executive corporate life at the age of 45, resigning from seven company Board's.

There was however a realisation that my family, of four great kids were not seeing their father and I was missing their precious early years. The liberating feeling of making that decision, that I was leaving the corporate world once and for all, was incredible and opened up an indescribable feeling of freedom not felt in the previous 26 years. It took me a further nine months to then leave my job, but the difference during that time was that my employer was now funding my exit plan rather than me 'working for a salary.'

My background of business, construction, strategy and problem-solving rapidly drew me to repurposing those skills and experience into something much larger and more powerful than a corporate role could achieve. My corporate role required managing infrastructure rollouts from £1m to £1bn but my new future would embed itself in creating massive shared value, huge return on time invested and enabling impactful change at a societal level.

Since scale has never been something to phase me, large-scale commercial conversion and developments quickly became a strategic goal, along with a select few of my long-term corporate fellow director and great friends.

Is there risk? Of course, there is risk in every walk of life, some we can control and others that can strike without warning, a force majeure, an act of God. Risk is not a dirty word and something to avoid, it is something to embrace, evaluate, manage, respect and above all seize the opportunity from within.

Two of the greatest personal qualities I have witnessed in my lifetime from those who possess great vigour and drive, are the ability to combine:

1. Humility with confidence – the ability to take your knowledge, experience, confidence and passion and to still remain humble and grounded in the knowledge that perfection is unattainable but the assessing and applying of the greatest minds will trigger the greatest evolutionary forces possible.

2. Anticipate and embrace change – don't run headlong into issues that could have been anticipated. Have the wisdom to access the vast experience of others that have gone before you and the agility to plan and drive whilst being flexible and tenacious.

These are rare, yet powerful qualities when merged creating exponential benefit.

The leverage, calibre and scale of the professional resources at our disposal enables us to deploy complex developments in a risk assured manner. It is that approach, process and systematic governance and compliance, coupled with entrepreneurial agility and tenacity, that has enabled our portfolio of businesses and strategic investments to grow into a life-changing multigenerational legacy for our families.

EquaGroup was founded on the principles of enabling and creating shared value from a societal, through to personal level. We combine our passion for business with a deep-rooted desire for our younger generation to understand the incredible opportunities and choices that await them outside of traditional guidelines that society often preordains!

My wish for this book is that it triggers the belief in you that every heartfelt desire you have is attainable if you are prepared to reach out and seize the moment, take the strain and embrace the journey. It can be a wild ride of emotion, anguish, choices and celebration but I promise you that every day that passes you will grow in stature, confidence and moral fortitude.

The Haircut

My business partner, Nigel Greene was walking into town for a haircut one day, and, as a savvy property investor of many years who is always looking up at the local property market rather than down at the pavement, spotted a sales board being fixed onto the side of a building.

Stopping to enquire, Nigel quickly learned that the building was coming on to the market for sale the next day.

A quick call to the commercial agent resulted in a returned call a few minutes later while he was sitting in the barber's chair!

Within two hours Nigel had secured a viewing of the property and by mid-day was touring the building.

The due diligence was quick to say the least that day, although we do know the area well, and after a quick conference call among the Directors of EquaGroup, our development company, we approved an offer and quickly submitted it during the afternoon.

"to deploy complex developments in a risk assured manner"

While the first offer was not accepted, the revised offer later that afternoon duly was and the fine development that is Oak

House was conceived!

From first sighting to offer accepted the entire process took seven hours!

The current owner of the office building had had the foresight to understand Permitted Development Rights, securing successful determination for eight two-bedroom apartments. Each of these apartments were between 88 and 95m2, which is fairly palatial for the target market.

Our strategy was to intensify the residential units by applying through Permitted Development Rights, for 16 x 1 bedroom apartments.

This duly took one week to prepare and 45 days to be successfully determined, adding great value within weeks of securing the development.

"100% of reservations taken within TWO hours of release!"

Case Study: Oak House, Colchester

Oak House was an 8,500 sq. ft. (790m2) gross internal area office building, with a planning classification of B1a which is for office use.

It is located in a beautiful part of old Colchester (which is one of the oldest cities in the UK) in an area known as the Dutch Quarter within 50m of the stunning Castle Park.

The building was constructed in the 1980s and was beginning to become tired. It was subdivided by the previous owner with plasterboard partitioning specifically to suit their business and how it had evolved over many years!

To give you an idea of the high level programme of events for this development, we achieved the following timescales:

Nigel had a haircut!	Oct	16
Conditional Exchange	Dec	16
Intensified PD	April	17
Legal Completion	June	17
Soft Strip	June	17
Refurbishment starts	July	17
Help to Buy approved	Sept	17
Marketing phase 1	Nov	17
Marketing phase 2	Feb	18
Refurbishment completes	March	18
Apartments sold	June	18
Investor funds returned	July	18

The development was a great success, with phase one marketing resulting in 100% of reservations taken within TWO hours of release! But more about that later in the book.

Financially the development was a great success too:

Gross Development Value	£2,683,000
Purchase Price	£900,000
Refurbishment	£850,000
Funding, professional fees etc	£350,000
Selling costs	£57,000
Net profit (pre-tax)	£526,000

Before Image:

Concept Images:

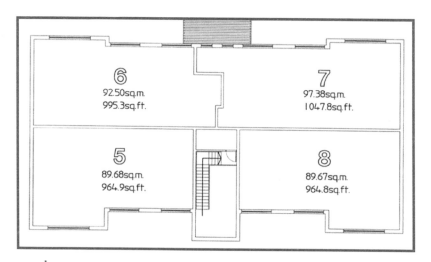

STEP INSIDE

With quality kitchens, oak finishes, clean lines and a contemporary palette creating an ambance that's both stylish and contemporary.

Our ambition is to build homes for the way people want to live today which is why each of the apartments are designed for practical living with beautifully proportioned open-plan layouts.

We are also committed to build homes of the highest quality that meet your needs. To show our commitment, all the apartments are finished to the highest standard and come with a 10 year building warranty ensuring long-lasting enjoyment and peace of mind for you as a new home owner.

During Construction Images:

Completed Images:

Those that know me well understand how I work and the ethos of EquaGroup. Success isn't left to chance and is the result of meticulous planning and attention to detail, anticipating every twist and turn possible and managing risk constantly.

Did everything always go right during the development? Well, despite its success we had challenges, after all, every development does, that is why we are so focused on risk management and have contingencies in many areas of our development appraisals.

Why this book?

This book is about the nitty gritty reality of the art and the science of commercial-to residential property conversions. It is a full immersion into what it really takes to achieve great success and outcomes.

We can all get excited about the profits and rightly so, however if the risk is not managed, the returns will vaporise.

I have wanted to write a book on this subject for many years now. My background is construction, operating global infrastructure programmes and running multiple companies, establishing, through intrapreneurship and entrepreneurship, new businesses and creating complex layers of shared value - a long standing passion of mine.

"full immersion into what it really takes to achieve great success and outcomes."

This book utilises my construction, refurbishment, property development, business and investment experience and combines that with the strategy of EquaGroup of commercial conversions and developments.

I wanted to create an engaging book for you where you can learn the crucial systems and considerations that will not only help you in your conversions but also help you to operate them as a BUSINESS.

The mind-set of operating as a business with the correct governance and compliance, resource optimisation, tax efficiency, well-funded and on solid business principles will provide confidence to both you and your stakeholders and enable you to have the courage and ability to scale your growth.

I want this book to help you towards a pivotal step in your life - to help you set out with the right business structure, philosophy, mind-set and approach as I take you through the 12 core fundamental steps any developer must take.

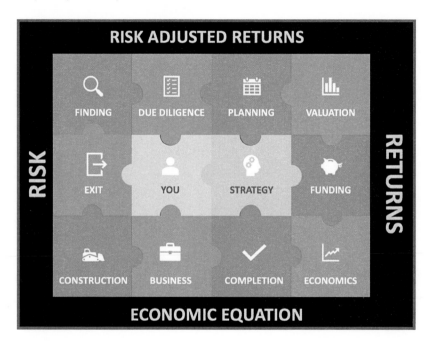

This will be invaluable for you to get started in commercial conversions and developments and guide you along the path to creating a greater risk-assured level of very meaningful returns.

It is not just what you do in life but also how you do it and how you make people feel - so whilst accessing these returns, you must be acutely mindful of the responsibilities and accountability

"It is not just what you do in life but also how you do it and how you make people feel"

that you have, the duty of care to your stakeholders, and the sustainable and professional manner you conduct your business affairs.

I am very firm believer that our reputation creates an indelible footprint, which in this day and age of social media, is under constant scrutiny by all. Like your business performance will be open to scrutiny, so will your performance in life and I hope this book will significantly advance your prospects in operating optimised companies where your commercial property and development schemes will create profitable returns and the creation of shared value for all your stakeholders, as well as yourself.

Who am I?

> *I demand from myself more than anyone else can humanly expect.*
>
> *I am competing with what I am capable of -*
>
> *Michael Jordan*

What defines us is often who we choose to spend our time with and for me that has absolutely been the case. I chose from the earliest days of my career to surround myself with some of the smartest individuals I could find. These have included friends, close working colleagues, mentors, fellow board members and others I have met all the way, from all over the world.

Three of my close friends and business associates are still my fellow directors after over 16 years. We have our own group of companies, EquaGroup, which Nigel Greene, Mike Tivey, Phil Burr and I have grown since leaving corporate life.

Nigel Greene   Mark Stokes   Phil Burr   Mike Tivey

I received my first class honours degree in Construction, from what was then known as Sheffield City Polytechnic in 1992. It is ironic that a career built on purposeful assessment started with a chance encounter, 'a sliding doors' moment at the end of my degree, where I went for a spur of the moment interview with a company I hadn't heard of before. It was an American Company called McCourt Kiewit International, a joint venture between McCourt Communications and Peter Kiewit & Sons. Subsequently, I became one of their first employees in Europe.

McCourt Kiewit International, later to become MK International, became the construction and infrastructure delivery arm, globally, for the large US and later global telecoms organisation, WorldCom, which is now Verizon. My responsibilities over that period of time, from joining in 1992, were immense to say the least, being dropped in at the deep end and thriving in a hugely fast moving environment. Those that sought responsibility were seldom left disappointed, and I remained a loyal and faithful corporate employee until 2002 in the aftermath of the Dotcom Bust.

"Those that sought responsibility were seldom left disappointed"

In 1992, I went to work in the United States with McCourt Kiewit International. I worked in a number of locations, including Chicago, Omaha and Dallas and spent the long and very cold winter (wind chill down to -40 degrees!) of 1992 at Lock and Dam #16, in Muscatine, Iowa, where we constructed a US$20 million refurbishment of the Lock and Dam infrastructure, on the Mississippi. That was an incredible opportunity to understand the complex world of joint ventures, in this case between ourselves as the main contractor and the US Army Corps of Engineers.

The project was a masterpiece of risk management, precision planning, health and safety as well as the civil engineering complexity that goes with working on frozen river systems, huge fleets of heavy machinery and explosives.

During my time in the US, I had the privilege of working at Kiewit Plaza, which is Peter Kiewit and Sons' headquarters in Omaha, Nebraska. During my stay there, one of my business colleagues and I went over to a restaurant in the local area and we were invited to share a drink and a bite to eat with another gentleman in the restaurant who my friend knew. We engaged in much conversation over the next couple of hours, and he duly left.

My business partner at that time asked me if I really understood who the gentleman was. I will say, at this point, I was 23 years old at the time and I had never heard of Warren Buffett!

I say this with humility and also looking back, reflecting on the laws of compounding it is not hard to start asking yourself questions based on: "If I knew then what I know now!"

At that point in time, Warren Buffett was worth $6 billion. Since 1992, his net worth has grown to $55 billion, exponential growth at anybody's level, but this

"I was 23 years old at the time and I had never heard of Warren Buffett!"

has been achieved through consistency over a lengthy period of time.

I started my career with MK International in the UK running large cable TV installation projects. I rapidly understood what it meant to be an entrepreneur, starting from scratch with very few resources and helping to build the organisation. I worked across England and Scotland extensively and into Ireland. At a similar time, I established a business which would go on to become one of the largest acquisition, design and build organisations of radio base stations in the UK for many of the new and emerging mobile providers, such as Vodafone, Mercury One2One and Orange, at the time in the mid 1990's.

We grew that business very successfully, but I reached a turning point in my career where I had to made a choice over whether to continue working with that part of the organisation, or seek opportunities with the parent company. I took the latter opportunity and ran the national infrastructure programme for very substantial data centres, in excess of £50 million in individual value and the nationwide rollout of the fibre optic network for WorldCom.

This then extended into wide-scale responsibilities across mainland Europe, from where I was then asked to take over operations and grow the Far Eastern interests of WorldCom and their global infrastructure deployment, in their Asia-Pacific fibre optic and data centre rollout.

So having only been married six months, my wife (Sharon) and I left the UK in 1999 to live in Sydney, where I worked for a couple of years in rolling out the infrastructure programme across countries such as Japan, Hong Kong, Singapore, New Zealand and Australia.

Imagine the change that had on our working and home life!

Previously my daily commute into London started at 5am with a two-hour drive to my office near Blackfriars in London and probably something approaching 2.5-3 hours back in the evening, arriving home around 8-9pm. My new role based in Sydney enabled me to live in the beautiful suburb of Mosman and enjoy a 20-minute drive along Military Road, across the Harbour Bridge and 'the sparkling bed of diamonds' which is Sydney Harbour, to my office in Piermont – what a contrast!

We came back to the UK in 2000, where I was responsible for rollout of fibre optic network infrastructure and data centres in Europe. By the end of 2001, the market had significantly changed and our organisation had direct instruction from the US to cease operations. My responsibility was to work with and lead a small hand-picked, elite team, to run the close-out operations of that business. I've built many businesses over my career and I have also had, what I consider a privilege, albeit a tough privilege, to close out businesses, whether that be restructuring, closure, or sale.

A huge amount of learning has been taken from these experiences. I've always approached those difficult decisions and situations by making them in a considered and thoughtful manner. Where staff have had to be released from the business, always be open and direct with them, explaining everything to them, be authentic and run a transparent process, while remaining compliant.

I've seen many emotions of people, whilst leading teams through change programmes, ranging from anger, tears, fears, uncertainty and gratitude. I remained true to my values of being open, personal and professional – it provides as much clarity as early as possible, a swifter transition, to enable people to move on with the rest of their lives. So the positives I can take from those situations, whether they be of growth or whether they be of closure, have helped me shape my approach in my professional career.

In 2002, my current business partners and I presented a business plan to a large, UK PLC, Mitie Group. Over the subsequent months of mid 2002, we established that plan and worked to create a new subsidiary company within the PLC. Mitie stood, at that time, for Management Incentive Through Investment Equity and we commenced our new business with a significant shareholding in the business, with us as significant personal investors.

We worked very hard on our company, which focused on design, build, and operations of data centres, for some of the largest blue chip organisations in the world. We grew this business very successfully and profitably, from scratch, from 2002 and eventually sold it back to the PLC in 2007 for a very substantial multiple of our original investment.

I would like to say the timing of this within the market was impeccable, however, I don't think any of us could lay claim to foreseeing what was to later unfurl in the global financial markets, in 2008 onwards.

From 2007, I then worked very closely with the PLC, in many roles. Those roles included mergers, acquisitions, restructuring, large development projects, renewable energy, power

"Calmness under pressure"

stations, data centres, as well as running construction, air conditioning, consultancy and engineering businesses. Passion for running businesses, working, and driving small teams to create a high performance culture has always been part of my DNA.

During the '90s and through to my departure from corporate life in 2015, I have seen a lot of challenges in business and overcoming those challenges has been core to gaining the experience I have today. I have always had to run a highly systemised business wherever I am, because one of my core roles at the organisations I worked for was as a corporate trouble-shooter.

My role would be, at very short notice, to be deployed wherever that may be in the world, to address a very significant challenge, work through that challenge, all the issues, with all the stakeholders and find a resolute set of solutions, that were palatable and amicable for all parties and resolve that situation through detailed investigation, understanding and proposals.

This proved extremely taxing, giving the wide-scale implications and indeed, many of these remain confidential to this day. However, the learning that was instilled in me through this process of working with people and understanding their reactions, as well as the technical and economic solutions, represents one of my greatest returns on time invested.

Two areas of valuable takeaway for me during these trouble shooting assignments were:

- The value of listening – I mean really intent listening, ask pertinent questions, assimilate information, digesting and act quickly.

- Calmness under pressure - When all around are emotional and panicking, diving for cover or laying blame, our team had to remain calm and collected, decipher the issue, the root cause analysis, negotiate positons and enable recovery programmes.

By 2014, I was starting to consider fundamental changes in my life direction. We have four children and the more successful I was in corporate life, the harder it became to spend the time that I wanted to spend with my loved ones - Ben, Jack, Katy, Emily and my wife, Sharon. Towards the end of 2014, I had discussions with my employer to engineer a sensible and logical exit that would enable me to pursue other ventures, whilst also fulfilling my corporate responsibilities.

During that transition period, we managed some more restructuring within the business and I exited, I am pleased to say, on favourable and professional terms.

In May, 2015, I left corporate life for the very last time.

I came from a very loving and hardworking family, with an immensely strong work ethic always being part of my upbringing and to be honest I have never lost that.

I was born in Boston General Hospital in Boston, Lincolnshire on

25th October 1969, making my presence immediately felt by being born breech - sorry Mum!

Always show the world your best side!

We lived in Boston at 60 Monteith Crescent until I left at 18 years old to study a BSc Construction at Sheffield City Polytechnic in 1988.

One thing that has always defined me from my earliest years is 'full immersion' into everything I was passionate about and that has never left me. Whether that was my first summer project on the Saturn V rocket at the age of 9, or my passion for snooker and later fishing.

If I enjoyed something, then it would become all-consuming – that was just me. My first job was stacking bar shelves and making sandwiches in the local Boston Snooker Club at Shodfriars. Needless to say my earnings were, in part, invested back into the light meter to play countless frames of more snooker!

Playing competitive snooker in men's clubs whilst still in my early teens was a great learning experience, where no quarter was asked for and certainly none given! I was there to prove myself on my own merits and I made an impression, winning league and individual trophies culminating in the Town Individual Cup – the Mowbray Cup - at 15 years old when I was so proud to have the cup presented to me by Len Ganley, a famous snooker referee at the time.

My fishing passion started at around 15 years old also and many a morning saw me jumping on my butchers bike with fishing gear heaped in the front basket to head off for another marathon fishing adventure with great friends - at 3am in the morning!

Match fishing became a staple weekend fixture and again immersing myself in adult leagues meant growing up very quickly and competing with the very best every weekend. Fishing is a rare sport where you can find yourself next to a World Champion on a Sunday morning!

"immensely strong work ethic"

This 'full immersion' has stayed with me throughout my life and this book may well be a by-product of that strand in my DNA!

In fact, over the 25 years of corporate life, where I bled loyalty for my company, I put everything into our business, often at a personal cost, although I probably wasn't fully aware of this at the time.

That is a natural default mechanism for me and I have had to work very hard, over the years to find the right balance – and maybe I don't achieve that very well. In fact, I am not so sure balance is something I really understand particularly well!

I like to combine my passion for my business and my commercial interests, with working hard to ensure that I spend the time that I really want with my children and my wife, achieving life goals.

I have also always tried to live my life 'to the max' and to create as many opportunities and experiences in life as possible. I want to live a life of no regrets. I have achieved a lot in my time, and experienced things which I'm incredibly proud of, always pushing myself to the limit.

Here are some of my personal highlights:

- Served my country in the Territorial Army in the 1990s
- PADI Advanced SCUBA diver
- Freefall skydiver - from aeroplanes and helicopters
- Mountaineering, snowboarding and skiing
- Rock climbing including free climbing
- Ironman Switzerland and Ironman UK (2.4 mile swim, 112 mile bike ride, and then run a marathon)
- Ran Thames Path 100 miles in 24 hours – turned out to be 107 miles!
- Ran 15 x 50+ mile trail races
- Ran Marathon Des Sables 2011

"Marathon Des Sables 2011"

When I competed in my first half Ironman, I finishing non-stop in 6.5 hours. Four weeks later, I competed in a full Ironman in

Switzerland. For those of you who know about training, you will recognise that you take one to two weeks to recover from a race and before a race, you have your taper training of one or two weeks. So between the half Ironman and the full Ironman, I had little time to train effectively.

During that time, it was important for me to rest and focus and with the right mind-set, I then looked at how could I achieve the full Ironman - from 6.5 hours to do a half Ironman and not being able to put another foot in front of me, to double that distance four weeks later. I estimated that, given the half Ironman took 6.5 hours, I would double that time and add an hour – not particularly scientific but should be a decent guide I thought!

"how deep is my reserve tank?"

So I targeted 14 hours. How then could I have possibly achieved my finishing time of 12.5 hours on the alpine course of Ironman Switzerland? Double the distance in less than double the time?

That got me truly analysing how deep is my reserve tank and the inner belief of why and how you achieve the goals that you set yourself. In truth, the swimming and the cycling was not a real passion of mine. However, I really enjoyed the running and in particular it was the off road trail running that really gripped me. Over the next six years, I became an ultra-endurance athlete, taking part in many races from 50 to 107 mile single stage events.

I also competed in a number of multi-stage events such as the OMM (Original Mountain Marathon) series of events and my largest achievement will always stand out as competing in the Marathon des Sables in 2011, in the Moroccan Sahara Desert, which has been referred to as "the toughest foot race in the world".

The race is a multi-stage event over 7 days covering circa 250km of some of the most hostile terrain ranging from 'liquid' sand dunes, fit for a Lawrence of Arabia film, to mountainous and rocky sections resembling a sand and gravel pit! With midday temperatures between 38 and 53 degrees the heat added to the grit of the event along with the rubbing and chaffing that comes with long lonely hours running in sand. One of the characteristics of an ultra-runner is that you definitely have to be comfortable with your own company! Maybe there is another book in me on this epic adventure one day!

In 1988, having passed my A Levels, I made a very late decision to not pursue a career in banking and decided to pursue a degree in construction, following my father's footsteps as an engineer. I applied through the clearing system, was accepted and then went to Sheffield City Polytechnic to start my degree in Construction.

I arrived in Sheffield with all the hopes and aspirations that any young man might have, with their visions of what was achievable in my life.

I had the opportunity in my first year, 1989, to go to one of the largest football matches I had ever been to, which happened to be an FA Cup semi-final.

The events that unfolded on that tragic day at Hillsborough in 1989 left 96 people dead and 766 injured, making it the largest disaster in British sporting history. The devastating events of that day left an incredible and profound mark on me and will haunt me to the day I draw my last breath. This, of course, is insignificant compared to the unimaginable suffering of those who lost loved ones and there will always be a place in my heart for them. It is something that is very hard to talk about to anybody, in fact, I locked the emotion away for over 25 years, not knowing quite how to handle the memories and trauma. The things that I saw and witnessed on that day will never leave me, nor be shared, they are too personal and will be forever in my thoughts - every face of those that perished and many of the survivors, as well as every noble act of courage from rescuers that I also witnessed that day.

Of the 96 people who died on that day, what many people are maybe not aware of is that 22 of them were between the ages of 10 and 18, arriving early to stand at the front to watch their heroes. Those young people never had the opportunity to understand life's riches, to have a vision and to make their mark in life and love; Life being cruelly snatched from them.

I believe a large part of my insatiable drive, in competing absolutely with what I am capable of and a lifelong quest to understand how deep my reserve tank truly is, has its origins from that day on 15th April 1989, which had such a harrowing impact on so many people. It created pain at a level that is incredibly hard to understand.

"that tragic day at Hillsborough in 1989 left 96 people dead and 766 injured making it the largest disaster in British sporting history"

Young Entrepreneur

*I don't think of work as work or play as play
it is all living -
Richard Branson*

The genesis of inspiring young entrepreneurs may have its roots back to April 1989, however the bringing to life of the potential only really surfaced after I retired from corporate life in 2015 at the age of 45.

I have a very healthy respect for the teaching profession and the great work schools do with limited resources. However, more needs to be achieved in instilling a passion and a drive in our younger generation to have a healthy respect for wealth – its creation, preservation and multiplication as well as cultivating and nurturing self-confidence to become an entrepreneur.

After all, in life, you can either be an employee or be the employer and very little in between.

"future generations will understand the life of choices that lay ahead of them, while still in their teenage years,"

I relish the possibility that future generations will understand the life of choices that lay ahead of them, while still in their teenage years, so that they can make decisions based on informed knowledge, rather than following the herd or only partial information about their potential options.

I am sure many of us as parents or grandparents would relish the opportunity to have had sage wisdom and counsel when we were in our teenage years, rather than learning the hard yards of life so many decades later – I know I would have!

Young Entrepreneur aims to support many young people to understand the life of an entrepreneur:

- WHAT it takes to succeed as an entrepreneur
- WHY being an entrepreneur can enable your talents to soar
- HOW to understand your potential and take the steps to realise a meaningful life of success
- WHAT IF YOU DON'T consider and what life might look like
- WHEN you can start to take action to live your life of no regrets

Young Entrepreneur initiative is supported by EquaGroup, an incubator of emerging diversity of talent and businesses.

Between our directors - Nigel Greene, Mike Tivey, Phil Burr and myself - we have 14 children and experience gained over 120 years of high-performance leadership and entrepreneurship, operating businesses nationally to globally, from business plan conception, start-up, growth, maturing, evolution and exit/asset disposal phases.

This has enabled us to have a deep and eclectic understanding of people, collaboration, what it takes to succeed in a changing world and enabling the highest calibre return on investment.

We are proud to 'walk the walk' as well as 'talk the talk' and three of our youngest budding entrepreneurs are employed in the business - Dan Greene, William Stokes and Tom Burr – all dynamic, aspiring, dedicated and talented businessmen in the making whom we are incredibly supportive of in reaching their full potential.

Whether you are a budding young entrepreneur or considering it, it is certainly never too late to access the exceptional life your desire, liberate your inner talents and enable you to connect with your purpose and goals.

The values that I believe are important to convey to our future generation include:

- Enabling an income mind-set
- Creating impact in the life of others by solving their problems
- Igniting the belief and desire to be the very best version of yourself

We look forward with anticipation to sharing some substantial initiatives that will continue to help our younger generation be inspired by the wonderful opportunities in life that entrepreneurship can enable.

Well Advised

Through running many complex businesses over many years, I understand the complexity and challenge of growth and the decision making processes that need to be made. As you develop your commercial conversions and developments, you will come across many challenges. There are risks that need to be navigated and you will need the right type of mind-set to approach those with the diligence required to mitigate and transfer those risks.

It is seldom possible to transfer all risks and the accountability of those risks in many cases will remain with you. However, with the mind-set of humility, I would suggest you will be able to carefully and thoroughly navigate your way through that process.

What do I mean by humility? Humility is one of the most powerful parts of business acumen and mind-set that exists. Arrogance can lead to complacency, however, humility will give you a strong foundation, the ability to take advice from all quarters, to understand what the options are and enable you to absorb information from all sources on your quest towards mastering your objectives.

When you possess the humility to know that you don't know everything, the natural consequence is to evolve your professional team and become "well advised." In becoming well-advised, you will have the very best team around you, you will avert growing a big overhead, but outsource to professionals far more qualified and experienced than you. Be sure to surround yourself with an extremely high calibre, well scrutinised and vetted professional team who will give you the sage advice you will undoubtedly need.

"Humility is one of the most powerful parts of business acumen and mind-set that exists"

Your challenge will be that different types of advice usually don't come in concert with each other. You are the conductor of your orchestra. You will have to make decisions. This is often missed by the entrepreneur. In becoming well advised, you may well be left with a number of pieces of conflicting advice. Can any of you relate to a situation where all you want is an answer from a professional advisor, but they give you snippets of advice rather than a recommendation?

I would encourage a very open relationship with your professional team and allow them to walk a mile in your shoes so they have the context of most situations to enable them **"you can never outsource crucial decision making"** to really understand what your true requirements are. Ultimately, you can never outsource crucial decision making. You will have to stand tall and make those calls, to assimilate the advice that you gained, and then make a decision on which route to go for and then instruct your professional team accordingly to move forward.

So where will you find your advice?

Three areas of advice that were given to me many years ago are as follows. Endeavour to be:

- Selective: Lots of well-meant advice from lots of quarters will often create a confusing picture which you will have to digest and percolate. At some stage you have to make the decisions to move your business forward, so make sure you pre-select your advice sources carefully.

- Relevant: ensure your advice is coming from those that are experienced in your field or part thereof. Advice must always be in context.

- Current: the externalities change, whether that is in legislation, tax, planning regulations, your personal circumstances or that of your business etc. Always keep your advice at a level where it can anticipate change to enable you to be ahead of the curve, forewarned and forearmed to evolve.

Your advice will come from specialists in several areas including:

- Professional Team – we will cover this is in the following chapters. However, this will include, but not be limited to accountants, tax advisors, solicitors, planning consultants, architects, design engineers, quantity surveyors etc.

- Mentors – Mentorship is a relationship where a more experienced or more knowledgeable person helps to guide a less experienced person. The mentor must have a certain area of expertise and the relationship is based on a learning and development partnership between someone with vast experience and someone who wants to learn.

As a consequence, selecting the right mentor is a very personal decision based on the expertise required and the results sought. It may be that a single mentor may not be able to support you in all areas of your development requirements.

In selecting your specific development mentor, these are some of the questions I would suggest mentees ask potential mentors (based on my 20 years of mentoring) whilst gathering your due diligence:

1. Will your mentor readily provide their time for you to get to know them over a coffee?

2. How many years have they been in the development business, in the capacity you need support?

3. How many years have they been a company director – check on Companies House. Minimum 3-5 years would be my view to support compliance, governance and experience.

4. How many developments have they completed?

5 What does their social media profile say about their character?

6 Ask to speak to their previous mentees.

7. How much accessibility will you get from the interaction each month?

8. Will they keep you focused on YOUR strategy or dilute you with THEIR strategy?

9. Will their counsel have a tangible or intangible effect on your

results?

10. Do you respect them?

Non-Executive Directors

"an independent view of the company that is removed from the day-to-day running"

What is a Non-Executive Director? The NED's role is to provide a creative contribution to the board by providing independent oversight and constructive challenge to the executive directors.

A NED is expected to focus on board matters and not stray into 'executive direction', therefore providing an independent view of the company that is removed from the day-to-day running. The phrase 'can't see the woods for the trees' is apt and while all boards have significant skills, humility to understand when additional support is required is a powerful part of seasoned business acumen. NED's are appointed to the board to bring:

- Independence
- Impartiality
- Wide experience
- Special knowledge
- Personal qualities

What are the key responsibilities of a Non-Executive Director? Directors should use their NEDs to provide general counsel, different perspective on matters arising, matters of anticipation, their strategic planning and areas of concern. They should also seek their guidance on particular issues before they are raised at board meetings. Indeed, some of the main specialist roles of a NED will be carried out in a board sub-committee, especially in larger companies. The key responsibilities of NEDs include the following:

- Strategic direction: A NED may have a clearer or wider view of external factors affecting the company and its business environment than the executive directors. Strategically a NED can provide unbiased, refreshing insight, questioning and informed contribution and acts as a constructive critic in looking at the objectives and plans devised by the executive team.

• Monitoring performance: Non-Executive directors should take responsibility for monitoring the performance of executive management, examining progress towards achieving company strategy and objectives.

• Remuneration: In larger companies, an NED might also be responsible for determining appropriate levels of remuneration of executive directors. In smaller companies, your NED will work closely with the executive team to examine compliance and offer insight and suggestion as to the approach required.

• Communication: Company Boards can benefit from outside contacts and opinions. A NED can help connect the business and board with networks, people and organisations who may complement the effectiveness of the company. A NED may also be requested to represent the company externally.

• Risk: NEDs should ensure the Board has the integrity of financial information, controls and systems of risk management in place and that they remain robust.

• Audit: A NED has an important role, as part of the board, to ensure that the company is accountable to its shareholders through a true and fair reflection of its actions, financial performance and that the necessary internal control systems are put into place and monitored regularly.

Creating Shared Value

Insanity: doing the same thing over and over again and expecting different results - Albert Einstein

Having engaged within the construction industry in many countries, there is a consistent factor that emerged in my observations on the culture and ethos. If I want to make more profit, then you will make less!! No wonder the construction industry is one of the most litigious sectors built on decades of adversity and questionable practices, although I am pleased to say there has been a marked increase in performance in this area over the last 10 years, although there is much progress still to make.

As developers we are establishing value – we are the catalyst and our actions have the opportunity to set our own culture and that is what we are doing within EquaGroup. We call this

"we are establishing value – we are the catalyst"

'creating shared value.'

When creating your business, your values will be its core foundation. They are not something that will sit on a shelf in your office. Indeed, as entrepreneurs we may not have an office at all, we may work from home and live a full mobile lifestyle. The values need to be deep within us as business leaders and embedded within our team, living and breathing daily - enshrined in our DNA.

They must represent, in my opinion, the creation of shared value in everything we do. A core fundamental for our development organisation, EquaGroup, is the creation of shared value to ALL of our stakeholders. In order to understand this more, let us examine more deeply who our stakeholders are in the world of commercial conversion and development.

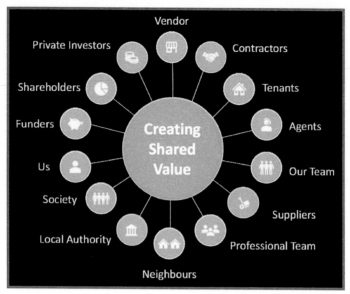

Our stakeholders are in every area which impacts our business and every area where our business impacts society. These can vary, but, as a rule, will consist of the following:

1. Our team

Our team are absolutely critical. We motivate our team, we inspire them and we create a culture of shared learning, shared knowledge, shared application and shared returns. Our team are crucial and will carry our vision to all corners of our business and industry as we professionalise every element of what we do in property investment and development.

2. Ourselves

As a business, we are in business to not only create shared value for others, but also to create value for ourselves as shareholders of the business and the responsibility of directors to run that business. We focus on operating a business rather than purely operating property. I would encourage you to consider the same; in fact, we will cover this in much greater detail in future chapters of this book.

3. Contractors

Our contractors are a core stakeholder in our business. We require contractors in our outsourced development model to provide the due diligence, the expertise, the ability to create the refurbishment and transformation of the existing buildings, which we are repurposing and regenerating to breathe life into ageing assets and create a new vibrant purpose that will sit impactfully in society. Our contractors are hugely important in translating the vision created by our professional team into reality. They will be responsible for doing this to the right levels of:

- Safety
- Quality
- Time
- Budget
- Compliance

"a psychology of creating shared value for our stakeholders"

4. Commercial agents

Our commercial agents are incredibly important in the process of establishing commercial conversion and development opportunities. We work very carefully with our commercial agent team. Our agents are professional, they understand the market and the transactions process. As we have said before, it is important to walk a mile in our stakeholders' shoes. From our commercial agent's perspective, they have an economic business model, which has a fixed overhead and they are paid generally on a success-based commission or fee. This fee is payable on completion of the property transaction.

We have a psychology of creating shared value for our stakeholders and understand exactly how they operate and how every element of the transaction process is important - and to whom. The commercial agent will favour our bid more than other parties' bids if we can demonstrate to them we have the credibility, track record, due diligence, integrity and rigour within our systems and processes, as well as our funding structure to enable surety of taking this development to a successful close of legal completion.

After-all, the worst scenario for a commercial agent would be for a developer to be unable to complete and the deal falls apart leaving the whole process to be restarted.

This is to be avoided as far as is reasonably practicable as you nurture your relationship with your agents. However, it goes without saying that only the correct due diligence and structure should be employed to ensure you are entering into the correct property transaction. Be very wary of compromises in your transaction process.

5. Suppliers

Your suppliers are a key stakeholder in your business. We outsource many elements of our business. Many will fall under the accountability of our main contractor, or our lead design team. However, you will have a number of suppliers and you will be reliant on them providing the quality and the exactness of their scope of works. Look after them, pay them on time, pay them a fair rate and they will serve you well into the future.

6. Professional Team

The professional team will enable you to structure your deals. They will also create governance and help enable your compliance at every stage. They will give you the assurance programme to understand the maximisation of value that can be created from your commercial conversion. They will work with you very closely through all stages and we will cover the professional team in a lot of detail in the chapters to come.

7. Neighbours

We include our neighbours of the proposed development as part of our stakeholders. A neighbour sits within society and with many of the properties we are considering, we are repurposing and regenerating these assets. These assets need a lot of tender loving care and attention and in many cases, their existing position is devaluing the neighbouring assets. So with the right type of approach and careful understanding, we can create shared value to the neighbourhood, which is incredibly valuable in supporting our planning applications and enabling our future buyers/tenants - our future custodians of our units when sold or let - to have a great start in their relationship within their future neighbourhood.

8. Planners & local authority

The local planning authority are also crucial and sensitive stakeholders. We work within the guidelines and frameworks set down by local government. However, the relationships that we have with our planning advisors, who are an essential part of our professional team, enable us to integrate with the local authority effectively and collaboratively where possible. The local planning authority are responsible for enabling the most appropriate scheme that works within the economic framework of our developments. We are very transparent with the local planning authority. They understand that developers must have a viable scheme. When they understand that actually our vision and values are around the creation of shared value, it can have a fundamental impact on how we work with them, how they entertain our schemes, our alternative suggestions, how we mitigate conflict and how we work collaboratively with them to find the right type of scheme that will create that shared value for society.

9. Society

Overall society is a core stakeholder; in fact, it is our target market where we are creating value. That value is in creating economically accessible high-quality homes for residents. The housing crisis that has beset the UK over many years now, through under-investment, is not set to be over any time soon. We are currently running at a shortage of 200,000+ homes each year.

Society MUST be a core stakeholder. It is the purchaser of our units and we must ensure our demographic, our product, our location all sit well within society.

10 Shareholders

The shareholders of our business are of primary stakeholder importance. We have, as directors, a fiduciary responsibility to our shareholders, a group that includes investors, members of our families and ourselves. It is important that all shareholder responsibilities are taken very seriously as we operate our business. We operate in the primary interest of our shareholders. These are economic from a cash-flow perspective, from a profitability perspective, from a growth perspective and indeed, from an overall sustainability perspective. It incorporates our moral and ethical compass bearing.

11. Funding Partners

These can be generally split into two sections:

• Commercial funding partners including senior debt, stretched senior debt, or mezzanine providers. These providers are important to our leverage and our ability to scale our projects. Banks have had a tough time in the past decade or so and I believe will continue to be held strongly accountable, quite rightly, for the decisions they make. We work closely with our commercial funding and development partners to understand their levels of compliance, probity and governance and make sure that we work closely with them to ensure fairness, openness and transparency in our transaction relationships.

• Private investors. We work with our private investors who bring capital to our business through loan agreements, or through private capital/equity injection into our company structures for our development projects. It is important that we understand and walk a mile in their shoes, understanding what great looks like to them and what type of value creation is high on their priority list. This varies from private investor to private investor and we will cover this extensively in the chapters to come.

12. Vendor

The vendor is a key stakeholder here and is pivotal in the process and a gateway to ensuring the further value creation to all of our stakeholders. We spend a lot of time with our commercial agents and with the vendor to understand their particular circumstances and how we can create a mutually agreeable and collaborate solution, whereby all parties are engaged in a deal which works for them. A great win, win, win strategy.

13. Commercial lease holders

Our clients who operate commercial leases within our commercial property are also a stakeholder. Some of our buildings will be of mixed use, having residential and commercial tenants. They may have been split through freehold/leasehold, but our commercial leasee's, the calibre of their covenant, the conditions of the lease and their performance during the period of their occupation will have a direct bearing on other stakeholders, both economic and societal. So our relationship and the creation of quality accommodation for our commercial leasee's, is high on our priority list also.

During my quarter of a century in corporate life running large global infrastructure companies and projects around the world, I have found that it has been invaluable to ask open questions at the appropriate time and to listen and truly understand "what does great look like to "you?" Only when one truly understands what the other parties in the negotiation or relationship values deeply and wants as a potential outcome, can one truly start to look at a viable proposition that works for all parties.

In my experience, particularly working with joint venture partners, this is vital to understand and enable swiftness of transaction. It is so important to walk that mile in other parties' shoes, to ask the tough questions during the good times in advance of sealing the deal. Negotiating with all parties is more often about listening and understanding, rather than talking.

There is a quote that says: "Negotiating is not listening to what they say but finding out what they want." You will not achieve this without firstly presenting the open questions and the environment of trust, to create openness. And secondly, listening to their feedback and truly understanding what their position and mind-set is.

"what does great look like to you?"

Anticipation

Don't let someone else's opinion of you become your reality

One of the core objectives of this book is to help you anticipate problems in the future. Benjamin Disraeli, UK Prime Minister (1874 – 1880) is quoted as saying; "What we anticipate seldom occurs. What we least expect generally happens."

A lesson for us all in the power of anticipation. This book is about opening your eyes to the risks, rewards, processes and systemisation that is required in commercial conversions, to help you address, understand the risks and the returns and enabling the safest routes to achieve those returns.

The power of anticipation and understanding what anticipation really means, is vital. All of your stakeholders have requirements. They will want to understand the why's, the when's, the how's. You will want to understand all the elements that they consider important to them. You will need to understand the market. You will need to anticipate potentially what the market can do, to anticipate the cost of money, to anticipate the process required, to anticipate the paperwork required and the diligence in advance, to anticipate the problems, the opportunity, and to anticipate some of the personal commitments that you have to make.

If you can anticipate all of those risks, the rewards and understand how they interact, then you will understand that the challenges are actually 'on the way' and not 'in the way' – it's a mind-set!

That is a fundamental entrepreneur mind-set which will help you to encapsulate and lock down not just the challenges but the

"challenges are actually 'on the way' and not 'in the way' - it's a mind-set"

opportunity to mitigate those challenges and to maximise and optimise the returns in your development.

Change

> *We cannot solve our problems with the same*
> *thinking we used when we created them*
> *- Albert Einstein*

Many people feel uncomfortable about change. However, change is probably the only certainty in life, after death. That is those that can anticipate, adapt and embrace change will create a far more robust and solid platform for their lives, rather than those who choose to remain subservient and reactive to change. They will always be behind the curve and striving to catch up.

With the high pace of change, the globalisation of business, rapid transformation of the economy and exponential technology advancement, we must remain on an ever evolving path continually enhancing and honing our skills and craft.

The technology space and software advancement is a great example of this. If we look at the rise of smartphones, which cost as little as $10 in some third world countries, more people have smartphones than have bank accounts. We only have to look at the rise of the Uber economy. With Uber, the largest taxi company that owns no taxis, Airbnb, the largest hotel company that owns no properties, Amazon, the world's largest global retailer that owns virtually no stock and likewise with Alibaba.

Each of these models is continuously being challenged. The disruptive model of Uber is now being challenged by new start-ups and of course the well-publicised legislative challenges in London, similar to Airbnb in Paris.

There are a number of significant changes in the ever evolving global business models but we can also see how the pace of change in harnessing, collecting and utilising data is transforming every marketplace on the planet - with large organisations like Google.

We also see significant changes in how society values effort. This change is extremely pronounced in areas where employers continually devalue effort. Effort is not a valuable commodity in today's society, I would argue, and increasingly the world is moving from an input-based economy towards an output-based economy.

The world wants to pay for outcomes, simple. If I use the analogy of a website designer, a client does not want to pay £50 per hour for a website designer - what they want to pay is £500 for a completed website. Outcomes are the future and any party prepared to be paid on an hourly basis is probably going to be disappointed in the future. The rise of computing capacity and artificial intelligence such as IBM Watson is growing exponentially. For instance in the US, an increasing number of legal practices are coming under very significant pressure because technology can create and search databases and understand logic better, quicker and far more accurately than the human brain can.

With the work we are doing to transform and help young entrepreneurs, we are also finding that the curriculum vitae (CV) of life is changing for our youngsters. No longer do employers wish to value how long somebody has worked somewhere. What they want to see is achievement and how that achievement has been incurred, as a sign of initiative. In fact, one of the largest statements one can make is to actually be your own economy. Be robust, resilient and be your own economy - safeguard your own future above anything else.

After all, once you are in the best position yourself, you are in a great position to help others. Change is always present in our lives. We must ensure that during the course of our commercial conversions and developments, we recognise that change is happening around us. The type of product we're offering will need to change

"The world wants to pay for outcomes"

to recognise the demands of our clientele, and the type of risk profile and appetite of our private investors and funders.

Business mind-set

*Negotiating is not listening to what they say,
but finding out what they want*

Most commercial conversions and developments, given their size, requirement for tax efficiency and the method of funding, will almost certainly be undertaken in a corporate legal entity which may be a limited liability partnership or a limited company, possibly others.

There are many reasons of efficiency, control and risk why we would establish legal entities for our developments. However, it ensures our mind-set rapidly transitions from that of a sole trader mentality to one of business acumen.

Businesses are not necessarily complicated. They just need to be understood and a clear system followed. A business mind-set will, firstly, need a clear understanding that YOU are a separate legal entity from your business. Your mind-set needs to shift in terms of understanding the risk and your position that you have within that business. You may be a shareholder or a director, or you may be an employee - you may be all three and each has a differing set of obligations.

"YOU are a separate legal entity from your business"

There is business acumen and logic that is required to ensure proper compliance, governance and probity. When you become a company director, you will have fiduciary responsibilities which must be adhered to.

Many businesses are very successful. However, statistics regularly show that in the first two years, there is up to a 75% failure rate in new companies. Ensure your business is grounded on solid foundations as very few go bust through lack of profit. Your cash flow is your fundamental. In the same way, your personal cash flow is crucial, your business cash flow will be a key determinate of the health of your business.

As a director, you will look at how you structure, what resources you have within the business, how you fund that business and how you comply with various tax and compliance requirements.

In commercial developments it is usual to have one development per company, which is referred to as a special purpose vehicle (SPV).

SPVs, sometimes referred to as an SPC (special purpose company), will be either a:

- Limited company
- Limited liability partnership
- Trust
- Charity
- Offshore company

Seek advice from your tax advisor, accountant and solicitor to establish the legal entity and structure that is right for your business. They will be able to work closely with you to assess not just the most appropriate structure for this company, but also how it integrates (or not) with your other companies to create the most advantageous position for the shareholders.

It is worth bearing in mind that some of your stakeholders may have more than a passing interest in this structure and entity. As an example, your development funder will take a different view on your company being a straight forward UK Limited company compared to an off-shore company registered in the British Virgin Islands.

SECTION TWO

THE 12 CORE CONVERSION PRINCIPLES

*Action may not always bring happiness;
but there is no happiness without action -
Benjamin Disraeli Smith*

The 12 Principles

Over the past 26 years of running businesses, construction and infrastructure projects, property investment and development **"we have created an economic framework"** programmes, we have created an economic framework, which will now help you to understand, anticipate and deploy your commercial conversions and development projects in the most secure manner, to heighten and optimise your returns.

We will take each of these 12 principles in detail to enable you a clear roadmap to be the best version of yourself and to manage your developments effectively.

1. You

You are the most important person in this process. It will be your vision, your drive, your agility and your tenacity to overcome many challenges, to anticipate challenge, opportunity and change, which will inevitably happen along the way. YOU will define YOUR outcome. Your mind-set, values and the way you approach and conduct yourself will have a very significant bearing on the sustainability of the shared value you are establishing.

2. Your strategy

Your strategy requires a careful thought process and detailed consideration. This strategy will be at a personal economy level as well as on a business level. You may have other business interests, other property developments, other property portfolios and you may be an employee. Understanding what your strategy is, why and what impact this might have on your capital and time, will enable you to shape your strategy.

How do we deploy our development strategy? Well, these further 10 steps as part of our 12 fundamentals will help you build your programme.

3. Finding

You will need to find the opportunity – they are not easy to find but they most definitely are out there waiting for you to uncover them. How do you find a commercial conversion? What resources do you need? What level of expertise and what level of scrutiny is required?

4. Due diligence

Due diligence, due diligence, due diligence and make that 'Bank Grade' due diligence starting as early as possible! Your due diligence must be detailed enough, bearing in mind the time and resources at your disposal. However, it's needs to be done quickly to enable you to work at a fast enough pace to capitalise on opportunities.

5. Planning

Planning is one of the areas where we force significant appreciation into the asset. However, there can be many opportunities and pitfalls awaiting the unwary so the process of planning is not just what you do, but the process you follow to achieve the desired outcome without incurring substantial downside risk along the way.

We will cover detailed understanding of the compliance aspects and the processes required, the cost, time and the likely outcome as you structure your offer and conditions and move through the various phases of your development.

6. Valuation process

The valuation process is probably one of the most feared processes in bringing your development to funding fruition. It is structured prescriptively and is fundamental for your funders decision making. Understanding the valuation process in detail will enable you to anticipate the process in advance by walking a mile in the valuer's shoes and then consequentially in the funder's shoes, to enable a smoother transition through this stage of your development.

7. Funding

Every project will require funding of one description or another. This can be broken into two core areas. We will examine the commercial funding and development finance market as well as securing private investment, compliantly.

8. Economics

We will look at the overall macro and micro economics of your development, your business and the externalities that can affect it.

9. Completion

The completion process is often thought about in terms of the conveyancing of the property purchase. We will be covering the additional processes of establishing your legal entity and the processes of on-boarding private investors and development finance.

10 Business

A commercial conversion will almost certainly be undertaken within a legal entity. The mind-set of running your commercial conversion as a business is fundamental to the successful outcome. The level of attention to key business fundamentals such as cash flow, operational efficiency and tax has been a determining factor in the failure or success for many businesses. The operating of your business in an optimised and efficient manner is important to enable your development to stand the best chance of achieving the successful financial outcomes, for not just you but also the creation of shared value to all of your stakeholders.

11. Construction process

Whether you are constructing new build or converting existing buildings, or a combination of the two, the construction process is not something to fear - after all it is visually where your hard work materialises! It is true that the scale of construction risk will increase on the larger projects. However, it is important to understand that the calibre of the professional team that you are likely to engage, including your main contractor, will also increase and your ability to manage those in the most prescriptive way, under a very clear contract of accountability and responsibility, will enable you to manage the development with compliance, governance and assurance. The construction phase therefore is not to be feared, however it requires structuring properly and then mindfully executing with the correct team, engagements contracted and audit programme in place.

12. Exit

Arguably the exit are your first thoughts when considering your strategy and will require at least 2 economically viable routes. Once the construction phase has been complete, we will be exiting the development phase. However, the detailed planning of the exit phase starts at the due diligence phase as it has fundamental implications as we will see on tax, funding, product and timescales amongst other considerations.

Our 12 principles cover the core areas for your successful commercial conversions. It is your economic equation, with success enshrined in the fundamentals, the details and the economics. Yes, there is risk. Risk must be addressed, acknowledged and understood right from day one, as well as viewed in context with the powerful returns that commercial conversions can hold for you. I encourage you to look at your risk-adjusted returns as part of your economic equation for your commercial conversions. We will now take each step in detail to enable you to complete your economic framework for your 12 principles of commercial conversions.

1. You

*Everything is impossible until someone does it -
Nelson Mandela*

While this is not a personal development book per se, it most certainly recognises the huge importance on the main driver and facilitator of this strategy – the person at the helm of the ship, its skipper – YOU!

As with any high-performance culture, whether that be Formula 1, world class ocean sailing, mountaineering or business, there are a number of facets which are incredibly important to consider. If you fail to encompass each one of these key elements into your Master Plan, you will come a CROPPER. The dictionary definition of "coming a cropper": Heavy fall tumble, disastrous failure, fiasco.

Follow these 7 steps to ensure you avoid coming a CROPPER:

- Clarity of Goal
- Resource plan – people & equipment
- Optimum personal conditioning
- Plan & programme to get you there
- People
- Excellence
- Risk Management

Let us take each one of these in turn:

1. Clarity of Goal & Vision

You must be clear and passionate about your goal – without this you will not be able to communicate your vision to others. Your goal should be large enough that it can stretch you and be of a long enough duration to not be just a short sprint, but a long-term evolution and compounding of multiple channels of effort, tenacity and expertise, over time.

Setting your goals is where you have the freedom to choose without boundaries or limitation – it is YOUR goal and one that YOU should be fully engaged, committed and passionate about.

Colonising Mars is the vision of Elon Musk and creating a world free of Malaria is the target of the Bill & Melinda Gate Foundation. Both are pretty bold visions, especially given that "Malaria occurs in nearly 100 countries worldwide, exacting a huge toll on human health and imposing a heavy social and economic burden in developing countries, particularly in Sub-Saharan Africa and South Asia. An estimated 207 million people suffered from the disease in 2012 and about 627,000 died. About 90 percent of the deaths were in Sub-Saharan Africa and 77 percent were among children under age 5." (Source Bill & Melinda Gate Foundation Malaria Strategy Overview).

So whatever your goal is, make sure it is connected to your passion, your 'why' and your purpose. It will take a huge effort to shape your goal into reality so make sure you have the stomach to go the distance, keep focused and always have a point of reference - a 'North Star' - to keep focused on your thoughts and actions with clarity and objectivity.

2. Resource plan – people & equipment

Understanding what it will take to achieve your plan is crucial to its timely success. This is where the power of anticipation will serve you well. You will need a plentiful supply of resources along the way, whether that be cash, equipment, people, systems, food, water, property and transport etc.

Set your awareness early on the variety and likely quantum of resource required and always add contingency. Many a plan has failed or gone over budget by underestimating the difficulty of the challenges ahead, leaving little latitude for flexibility.

3. Optimum personal conditioning

"Small Is Beautiful: Economics as if people mattered" Take care of yourself. It is easy to become self-consumed and forget about being in the best shape, both mentally and physically, yourself. A Formula 1 driver is as crucial a part of the overall team effort as the design engineers for the car itself. In fact, an F1 driver is one of the fittest athletes in world sport, having to constantly withstand and operate at the highest level whilst under constant 3-5G lateral forces to the body, for several hours at a time, as well as the relentless practice and training. I know from personal experience it is easy to become self-consumed in the objective and to lose sight of your physical performance which, in time will manifest itself in a reduction in performance, energy and focus if not addressed early. Make this a key part of your routine.

4. Plan & programme

Every goal must have a masterplan which brings the entire strategy together, including very clear timelines on what is required, by whom and when. It will ensure that your team understands the part they play, the dependencies their particular element has in the success of the overall venture and the urgency, tempo and timing of the route to the end objective.

5. People

This may not be what you are expecting. We covered people as a resource in 2, above. 'People' in this context is making the thoughts, hopes, aspirations and generally "what does great look like to you?", of other people, in context with and aligned to your plan. Every plan has stakeholders and it will serve you well to understand what makes every part of your team tick, to enable all parties to be as motivated to achieve the end goal as you are.

The great 20th Century economist EF Schumacher wrote a compelling masterpiece seen by many as ahead of its time – "Small Is Beautiful: Economics as if people mattered". In this seminal work, Schumacher makes a very valid point that economic prosperity does NOT have to be at the expense of people, the environment or natural resources and indeed they can all co-exist harmoniously. In this strategy we have a huge opportunity to demonstrate this to stakeholders, in many areas and indeed within EquaGroup this stands as one of our core drivers.

6. Excellence

Mediocrity is a disease and this mind-set must be avoided. Excellence in all we set out to do and achieve will enable the high performance culture, which is much more likely to bring about high quality results. Accessing the very best knowledge in class for your development is a must and applying it in a critical yet specific manner, will aid your route to achieving your goal. However, the accumulation of knowledge is only a small part of the story. Your considered application of that knowledge is what will define your outcome. A great example of this is getting the right advice from professionals – I cover this in a later chapter. It is a frequent position that many find themselves in where their professional team are giving them lots of well-meant advice; however, the one thing you cannot outsource is decision-making. There comes a point in any process where enough knowledge and advice is in your hands. You must avoid procrastination and make the decision that will take you forward.

7. Risk Management

Much of what we discuss in this book is the professionalism of risk management through bank grade due diligence. Successful conversion of opportunity lies at the heart of being able to manage risk and therefore risk should not be seen as a dirty word but rather something that is omni-present, to embrace and manage actively.

The mind-set around risk comes in 4 basic approaches:

1. Identify – you have to identify the risks in the first place through thorough analysis.
2. Mitigate – find different ways to do tasks/operations to reduce risk levels.
3. Transfer – find specialist parties who are better able to manage risk than you are.
4. Manage – After you have managed the steps above then you will create plans to manage any residual risk remaining.

The Brand of You

You are your number one asset in life and in business and your reputation is the most valuable component of that. It is the brand of You. Everything you do, say, how you make someone feel will enhance or erode your personal brand. The brand of You is with you for life and is formed in the minds of others at every stage and interaction with you.

Professionalism is incredibly important in business. However, I would also add that being personal is a great trait in development as this is a very people focused business strategy.

"You are your number one asset in life"

Your reputation is the hallmark of everything you do, it enshrines your very ethos. It is built up over your lifetime - those that know you, know you by your actions and your history – this is nearly impossible to fake over the long term, although many do seem to try!

It is hard to build a solid reputation. It only happens through dedication and action. It is also incredibly easy to lose.

Elements of your reputation by which others may assess you may include:

- Character
- Personal traits
- Humility
- Integrity
- Values
- Passion
- Drive
- Approachability
- Wisdom
- Success
- Wealth – in all its forms

Your reputation is not judged by you, but rather an opinion gathered by others, based on performance over time, a single act, perception, word of mouth and crucially today within your social media footprint.

Input to output based economy

The world is changing exponentially. Do you want to be judged on how hard you work or what you achieve?

A strong work ethic sits at the heart of success without doubt. However, society places less VALUE on hard work and people care less on how long you work. What they DO care about is what you achieve and deliver.

As entrepreneurs we have now well and truly moved from an Input-based economy to an Output-based economy.

In the 20th century, society predominantly recognised and rewarded hard effort. Jobs for life were available and loyalty of workforce was recognised as a badge of honour by employees and employers alike.

I know people who have worked for the same organisation for 50 years. It is difficult to comprehend the economic circumstances that would enable that to happen these days.

Let us look at the traditional employee CV. I would hazard a guess that the vast majority celebrate the company, the role and the duration of employment and from an employer's perspective, too many employers on a CV typically may indicate an unstable or unsuitable employee!

It tells you a lot about what employers value and how society is changing exponentially.

Celebrate Equality & Diversity

One thing I have learned over the 26 years of corporate life and life in general, is to celebrate the diversity and contribution that comes with equality at a deep and meaningful, societal level.

We have set equality & equitability right at the heart of EquaGroup of companies, which sits proudly in our name and logo.

The richness of knowledge, opportunity, collaboration and inclusion that comes with embracing the very best of the best, irrespective of background and belief, is a potent force in achieving pioneering and exceptional competitive advantage, as well as being a great social citizen and valued member of the human race.

Some of the areas which are frequently held as inner prejudices by some include gender, race age, disability, background, religion and sexual orientation etc.

I have shared with you my passion and very personal reasons for wanting to inspire Young Entrepreneurs. This drive is to open out the wonderful world of opportunity to entrepreneurs at a young age, to challenge convention and tradition and strive to take control of their own personal economy. To make their mark on life at an early age, enabling them to reap the benefits over time and to repay society by continuing to pass on their accumulated knowledge to others, affording them a similar opportunity to succeed and share with others.

Leadership

In life you can either be a leader or a follower. The independent thinking of a leader who knows his or her mind, yet has the wisdom and common sense to establish the best course of action based on sage advice, is a wonderful combination.

The great traits of leadership have been well documented over the years but the ones that stand out for me include:

Vision – leadership requires a vision broad enough to accept change along the way, yet clear and precise enough to be attainable.

Plan – clarity of the steps to attain success of the plan and vision, turning into a roadmap of what is required from who and when.

Courage – leadership can (and often does) mean making tough decisions. You will not please all of the people all of the time and the end goal has to remain in clear focus. Courage is making the correct decision at the right time, from the right advice and being able to inform the team so that they are clear, irrespective of 'opinion engineering' that may exist. A strong backbone is essential.

Communication – this lies at the heart of much of a leadership role. Communication is often not just what one says but also how one delivers the message, what one does, body language, method of communication and much more. I have had the privilege to work alongside many great leaders and they have all had very different styles. However, their method of constant and consistent communication is what set them apart as great leaders.

Humility – a leader must remain humble at their heart, being prepared to embrace best advice, knowledge, skills and people in order to grow. Humility is the ability to understand that the improved success will come from embracing the 'greater than the sum of the parts' synergistic approach to gaining best in class.

Challenge – a leader challenges convention, looking for the best in class performance and innovation that will drive competitive advantage, aiding the growth and security of the organisation's positioning. A leader must be prepared to challenge everything and to be challenged on everything – but to also know when a decision needs to be made and to make it.

Accountability – leadership is from the front and visible, it is demonstration by action and is where the 'buck stops'.

Passion – leaders live and breathe what they do, you can't fake it, it is part of your DNA and belief system and is expressed in everything you do.

"establishing a culture where the best talent, ideas and processes are brought to the surface on merit and actively encouraged and incubated"

Focus – leaders know how to focus – they understand that maximum effort and application of intellect and resource must be applied to the goal.

Anticipate change – Leaders must be aware of, expect and embrace change. The art and science of anticipation will help you navigate the choppy waters and prepare your team and business for the good, bad and indifferent times ahead.

Compassion – understanding that there are ramifications and impacts from our actions to a wider society and having the compassion and understanding that these must be understood and managed too.

Meritocracy – establishing a culture where the best talent, ideas and processes are brought to the surface on merit and actively encouraged and incubated. This will create a wealth of continuous improvement. The best in class will always be encouraged and allowed to rise to the surface, irrespective of origins. Some of the best organisations and teams on the planet have grown exponentially based on this ethos. "Principles" by Ray Dalio is a great book which covers this subject comprehensively.

Your goals

Without specific goals, business and life can be rudderless, leaving little or no direction and no concentration of effort to achieve any one of several meaningful things. Time and direction can meander unless they are applied to a clear roadmap on how to get to the goal.

I like to set myself large goals of scale and ambition. As the old saying goes: "aim for the stars and you might hit the moon". Well I tend to disagree! If I am aiming for the stars, that is what I want to hit! My mind-set is: if I set myself a goal, then I have already mentally achieved it – I now just need to piece together the mechanics to get there.

So make those goals large, massive even and enable your own psyche and mind-set to adapt to a more expansive and open-minded thought process which will enable you to be drawn to larger opportunities that may exist.

In corporate life the common mantra regarding objectives was to make them SMART. For those who have not heard this before, SMART goals are referred to as:

- Specific
- Measurable
- Attainable
- Realistic
- Timely

BEWARE, BEWARE, BEWARE!!

As a property developer and entrepreneur, make sure you are not swayed by popular convention from an employee mind-set. You MUST make things happen and NOT be channelled by thoughts of an employee mind-set.

Your HR department may have included these SMART objectives on your annual performance review for instance. I cannot imagine something worse than being asked to define goals that were the

"A" = Attainable and "R" = Realistic!

Talk about capping one's potential and sowing the seeds of limiting belief!

encourage a "boundaryless" culture

Far better for us to encourage a "boundaryless" culture (a phrase coined back in the 1980/90's by Jack Welch, Chairman and CEO of General Electric) where our achievement and personal stamp on this planet can be positively limitless!

Once your goals are set then you can create the roadmap to meet them. Do bear in mind that the world is moving at an exponential pace so make sure your goals can sustain the test of time. For instance, there may be little point in aiming to own a TESLA Model X in the next 10 years as the entire Electric Vehicle market will have advanced at an incredible pace during that time.

Your goals can be set in many areas of your life and at short, medium and long term ranges. They can include:

1. **Health & fitness** – How do you want to feel and look? What do you want to weigh? What do you want to achieve and enjoy? Understand what defines true health to you.

2. **Travel** – Do you have goals to travel? Where, when and how?

3. Relationships – Who do you want to live with? Where and how? What type of partner do you want to be?

4. **Parenting** – The example, legacy and custodianship you will invest and impart to your children.

5. **Emotional** – How do you best like to feel? Will you be in control of most of your circumstances? Will you be content, happy or continuously pushing the boundaries?

6. **Financial** – What will be your financial wealth - at what level and over what timing to ensure your financial security? How will you measure this and maintain its security across which asset classes?

7. **Intellect** – How will you continually challenge yourself to

grow and develop? Will this be by research, reading, your friendship groups etc?

8. **Material** – Will you measure your enjoyment through material goods such as cars, your home, boat, plane, clothes, watches etc?

9. **Spiritual** – Your spiritual positioning and practice, whether that be religious or state of mind.

10. **Social** – The friendship circles and activities you would like to experience and the type of person you wish to be.

11. **Giving** - Your larger grander contribution to the planet and to others. What will be your indelible legacy for future generations?

12. **Quality of Life** – The ability to live your life on your own terms, however and wherever you choose.

Measure & Monitor

Finally, it is essential that you measure your progress regularly to ensure you remain on track to achieving your long-term goals, while also meeting short-to-medium term goals.

The short-to-medium term goals will be quite specific and tangible and should be something you can visualise easily; however, it is still easy to be blown off course so continuous checking is crucial.

Be prepared to make micro adjustments along the way and to amend your goals if circumstances change. On this note, make sure that you keep an eye on the macro wider context of society and life.

Many things can change in the wider context which are outside of your control, hence watching government policy, politics, the economy, interest rates etc are an important part of identifying where changes may need to be made to:

• Manage risk

• Seize opportunity!

Pause for thought – The Power to Say "No"

Have you ever gone along with someone else's 'great idea' even though your gut told you not to? Afraid of hurting their feelings, didn't know how to decline, was afraid you might miss out?

I suspect you are not alone and most of us have done this!

As entrepreneurs we experience people saying "no" to us regularly. We tend to see failure differently to most - more a part of life's evolution rather than an abject situation.

Could it be that because of this, subconsciously we can also grow an all too unhealthy 'Fear of Missing Out' and end up saying "Yes" to too many things?

Our single most scarce commodity is our TIME - yes we can leverage others people's time but our own personal bandwidth of time and mental capacity is finite.

We must guard it with a passion. If we do not respect it, others most certainly will not and worse still, will come to expect our time unconditionally!

The power to say "no" is not a natural act, it needs to be learnt and mastered to decipher what is congruent to your main objectives, (whatever they may be) and what is not.

Many people find rejection hard, let alone GIVING rejection and yes, that is what saying "no" is.

In life it is not just what you do, but also how you do it….

So how might we decline someone else's perceived 'opportunity' while being courteous yet clear and maintaining our reputation?

These four clear areas will aid your clarity:

1. **Be clear, concise and honest** - explain the context of what you are doing and how this opportunity and its merits will not fit with your current plans.

2. **Be decisive** - Be respectful of your time and theirs and don't delay on explaining your decision.

3. **Be supportive** - offer advice to someone else who may have an interest.

4. Revisit - explain that the timing currently does not work and suggest revisiting the opportunity at some point in the future if it could be of interest.

To be efficient in how we say "no" and indeed what we might say "yes" to, I have found a useful framework of decision-making criteria works well:

- Does it feel right?
- Do I connect well with the people?
- What value can I provide?
- What would I gain?
- Is it what I want to do?

By saying "no" we remain on course for:

1. Doing the things, we want to do with our time
2. Focusing on the things that matter to us
3. Not compromising our true passion
4. Not diluting ourselves or deluding others
5. Reducing opportunity cost

Respect for ourselves is the first building block of any committed person. Respect your time and its impact - govern it wisely. It will pay you an incredible return on investment.

2. Strategy

*Great things are not achieved by those who count the cost of every thought -
Isambard Kingdom Brunel*

It is important to have a very clear understanding of what your personal and overall overarching property and investment strategy is, and why – the purpose it serves. As we can see from the image below, your strategy for investing particularly in property can be undertaken at various levels, whether that be on a buy-to-let and rent-to-rent basis, serviced accommodation, houses of multiple occupation, co-living, flips, small developments, commercial conversions and larger developments. Each one of your property strategy options will have a different risk profile and you will need to assess the calibre of your own ability to manage risk, your personal appetite for risk and the structuring of your business to manage that risk.

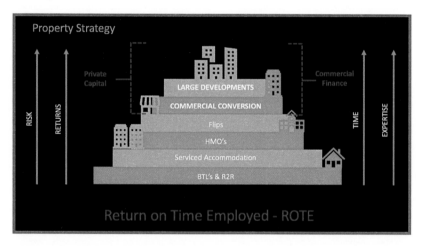

You will need to ensure that with risk comes return – focus on your risk-adjusted return strategy. Decide what return you are looking for and what form that return will come in e.g. income or capital. Look at the time that you have available to deploy your strategy. Is time a scarcity for you? Or will you have to bring in expertise inevitably to support whichever strategy you deploy? The expertise level that you require will be very different for each one of those strategies and therefore, the cost will vary tremendously. It's important for you to understand how you will manage the risks of your chosen strategy.

"focus on your risk-adjusted return strategy"

Your personal goals are really important to understand as your aspiring business goals must work in tandem with your overall personal strategy. What is your strategy? Will it be for the capital growth, a hold strategy for income, yield or sell with planning gain etc? Will it be to create working capital and reinvest strategy? Will it be a hybrid of different strategies? Will it be an income-generating strategy based on scale over time? Will it be working with other different vehicles, maybe pension vehicles such as SIPP and SSAS?

In commercial conversions it will be necessary to scale up the expertise you have at hand. You may well be able to build the property refurbishment programme yourself or manage lots of individual trade packages, but your commercial lender will almost certainly not accept this as there is little, or no, security behind this and no covenant strength. Funders and investors are looking for assurance through proven track record, externally accredited practices, professional indemnity insurance and ultimately step-in rights later down the line, should the worst case happen and the development fail. They are not interested in just backing you 'trying really hard' – after all what if you get hit by a bus tomorrow?

'Nickel-and-diming' the development can have serious implications on your ability to move forward with commercial lending and we will cover this in more detail in that section of the book.

Costs and how you are going to manage them, what are those costs? Can you forecast them? Can you anticipate them?

Credibility is important. Your personal and company CV should be enhanced to ensure representative skills that you have are translated into a document of assurance for your funding provider. This may also be a useful document when working with your private investors so that they understand what

'Nickel-and-diming' the development can have serious implications

"The development is usually a vehicle to get to your goal"

you bring to the table and your level of personal assurance.

Consider the tax effectiveness of your strategic decisions as they can have a bearing on your risk adjusted returns. As an example, the benefit of capital allowances on a buy-develop-and-sell strategy will be entirely different on a buy-develop-and-hold strategy.

When placing property commercial conversions and developments as your core strategy, you're entering into a world where there are serious commitments for you personally, irrespective of what legal entity you are utilising.

Finally, ask yourself whether the development you are pursuing is a goal in itself or a vehicle. Let me explain. If your goal is to achieve £X amount of capital or £Y amount of income, then the development isn't the goal. The development is usually a vehicle to get to your goal. If the development objectives are to create credibility for the future, then again, this development is a vehicle. Whilst your development is extremely important - and I'm not belittling that in any way - you must understand what the longer-term objectives and goals you have in your strategy and how the development fits into your framework.

3. Finding

*He who says he can and he who says he can't
are both usually right – Confucius*

The Right area

In the surge of emotion of trying to find the right building for you, it is a tempting mistake of the beginner to try to find the building that works and ignoring the area that it is located.

So what are we looking for in the location?

As the old saying goes 'Location, Location, Location' will be the single largest determining factor on the viability of your development. While we are not looking to live in the homes we are creating, it is important for the developer to 'walk a mile in the customer's shoes', to evaluate whether they would like to live in the area or indeed what the readily available alternatives are in the market locally of course! The basic Maslow hierarchy of needs is worth mentioning here as it holds true to most within society. The core basic needs are:

- Physiological needs: food, water, warmth and rest
- Safety needs: security and safety

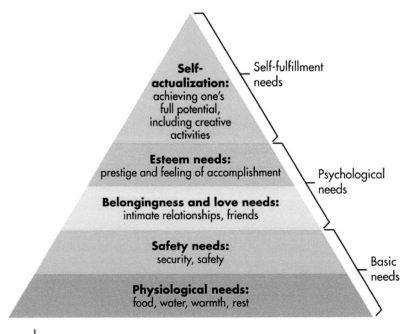

Our location should encompass both of these in our assessment.

We have evaluated hundreds and hundreds of properties over the years and experienced many poorly and inappropriate considered examples.

A recent example was a Permitted Development scheme in Berkshire, located right at the end of an industrial estate which had every light to medium engineering and industrial process operating, often on a 24 x 7 x 365 basis. While the building in isolation appeared to have all the right characteristics, the location was wholly inappropriate for our target market and we wasted little time going into any detailed due diligence as the location did not pass the acid test for us.

At our EquaGroup development at Oak House in Colchester, you can see from the map below the local area in some detail which benefited from being in the famous old Dutch Quarter, 30 metres from the beautiful Castle Park and only a five minute walk from major transport links and the local shops. Our sales levels fully supported the decision to develop in this area with our initial phase one release of apartments being reserved within 2 hours of release to the market!

"phase one release of apartments being reserved within 2 hours of release to the market!"

Amenities

Your customers, whether they are renting or buying your apartments or houses, will need to feel local to their requirements. Are local amenities within reasonable accessibility? These amenities might include:

- Shops and high street facilities
- Restaurants
- Recreational areas – parks, football, rugby grounds
- Gym/leisure facilities
- Employment
- Doctors/dentists

Transport links

Are you clear about how important transport is to your target demographic? Will they own their own car? Increasing numbers of young adults are preferring to not own cars now and adopting the 'Uber' lifestyle! Will they prefer public transport? Some of the main transport considerations to make include:

- Is car parking required?
- How local is 'off site' parking?
- Are bus routes close by – if so, how close?
- How far is the local train station?
- Is it a branch line or main line?
- Is there a local tramline or underground – if so, how close?

The Land

A view from above can help us assess the viability of land in the area prior to our site visit. We are generally looking at areas of population density to support our exit sales or rental strategy, hence the commercial property we are looking to convert and develop may well be in urban and town/city centre locations.

The benefit of planning to our development can hold a lucrative potential for us in enabling the otherwise unfulfilled potential of back land developments of rear gardens for example.

In a recent development that we secured in Essex, the former D1 care home had a prominent High Street location which was neighboured by a previous new-build development of five new-build homes. This insight enabled us to not only secure planning for converting the care home into four two-bedroom apartments, but also to gain planning for four new-build houses in the rear garden.

You will need to engage a specialist planning consultant to ensure you navigate the appraisal of your development carefully, protecting yourself with conditionality of offer where appropriate. Significant value can be created if this is done carefully.

There will be a number of factors to consider in ensuring hidden gremlins are not lurking. Inner town/city land will most certainly have had prior uses over the passage of time so your searches, enquiries and investigations should be very thorough.

Case Study – Colchester

The land, where a purpose built commercial office block was constructed in the 1980s, was previously used as a car service centre. No evidence could be produced that the new-build property in the 1980s had safely assessed and removed any ground contamination from oil/petrol etc.

This issue was raised in our searches and our view was that if we can find this issue, our apartment buyer's solicitor's would also be able to find it, hence it was very important that we delayed our exchange of contracts until we had finalised this query to our satisfaction. This would then pave the way for a streamlined sale of units and a swift exit from the development, due to minimising as far as possible any search queries.

While insurance etc might have been available, the only clear way to assess the risk was to take soil samples. We decided to employ a specialist to bring in a low head room drilling rig into the covered car park under the building and drill soil core samples through the slab of the ground floor car park and have these soil core samples sent for laboratory analysis.

While this process took a month, we then had a clear set of test results that could be identified on any future searches on the property, by future buyers. What was the cost for this investigation? In the region of £5,000 but the certainty of sale when in context, the senior debt interest costs could be running at £10k's per month, was well worth the investment of time and cost to remove any potential issues before we started.

The ability to be able to put your head on your pillow at night and sleep easy should not be underestimated!

Neighbours

Would you like to live next to that? You will have to make an assessment on the operations of the neighbouring property and not just what it is, to ensure that your buying market will not be put

"The ability to be able to put your head on your pillow at night and sleep should not be underestimated"

off and your apartments struggle to sell.

As an example it may be a light industrial unit beside your commercial conversion which could be acceptable to your future buyers, but if the day-to-day operations are running from 0700 – 1800hrs seven days a week with heavy vehicle deliveries and noisy operations, this can throw an entirely different perspective on the property.

Environmental

In addition to the local environment considered in this chapter, we must also be aware of the other environmental considerations which might apply. These may include:

- Local transport movements
- Noise
- Flooding
- Natural habitat – bats, newts etc

Careful consideration with specialist advice will be essential in producing a full impact assessment if these are likely to be an issue. Your planning consultant and professional team will be of invaluable assistance in this area.

History

History may not necessarily mean recent history!

Another of our developments in Essex is in a local conservation area and while full planning permission was achieved, it had the condition attached that an archaeological survey would be required prior to any works commencing.

In this particular case, the local area has been occupied since Roman times so the potential for unwanted surprise 'finds' may exist.

The uncovering of old castle ruins or a monastery, whilst a wonderful treasure for the local community, is not exactly considered a great day in the life of a developer and their shareholders!

Recent developments

Keep up to date with local planning and proposed developments. This is a fast-moving area and it is essential that you remain fully aware of the developments, in your area that may provide competition to your current developments as well as alter your thinking on supply and demand elasticity in the local area.

With an overall national housing shortage set to continue for many years to come, it is highly likely that government initiatives to stimulate the production of more homes through planning policy is set to continue. We have seen from 2013 – 2017 that Permitted Development Rights are being flexed to enable more developments. This will open up more opportunity for the developer and more competition, hence your due diligence can never stop even after securing your development.

The right building for your strategy

Once the right area has been considered then the right building can be assessed for that area. There will be a number of key considerations that may assist in maximising opportunity and minimising risk.

Roof

There are many considerations for the roof on your building: Is it pitched, flat, good condition, modified, does it have dormers or Velux style windows?

Another consideration is the height of the roof in comparison to neighbouring rooflines. This can provide us with an opportunity to take advantage of the 'air space' above the building and seek a planning gain by adding an additional storey(s) to the building.

This would most certainly require full planning permission under planning guidelines at the time of writing, however there has been consideration that Permitted Development Rights may be extended further to include the expansion into airspace under certain conditions.

This is yet another area for developers to watch carefully with their planning consultant.

"always work with the end in mind"

As we should always work with the end in mind, we must ensure that our end product can be sellable or re-mortgageable. Either way the buyer or your re-financier will be looking for a Structural Building Warranty on the apartment or house.

The provider of the Structural Building Warranty may only provide the warranty at the end of the process, after signing off with confidence that the roof will be acceptable for a 10-15 year guarantee.

Depending on the structure of the roof, it may be possible to extend into the roof void without particular modification to the external profile of the property, especially if Velux style windows are employed and/or existing roof void windows are utilised.

The make-up of the roof members will have a determining factor on costs from a structural perspective, depending on whether the structure can bear the additional imposed load on the building and whether the roof is primarily lightweight roof trusses or of a bespoke nature, capable of additional expansion.

Your design and planning teams will best determine what is in the art of the possible, leaving you to determine which risk/reward profile you are comfortable for your development.

Case Study: Creating space out of thin air

In a recent development within EquaGroup, we were able to turn a unique feature in the roof into a very positive advantage.

The development consists of 24,000 sq. ft. of B1A office space which we secured determination under Permitted Development Rights for 26 apartments and 2 retail units.

Running through the core of the building is a light-well which comes from the main roof down through the centre of the 4 storey building to the first floor.

We recognise the valuable asset of natural light in any residential scheme and duly applied for parallel planning permission to open up an interesting feature of 'dummy' windows in the existing facade into actual windows, thus enabling light to flow into the building and enabling us to remove the light-well feature.

We placed structural steels across the light-well feature and infilled at each floor, creating an additional 60m2+ of valuable floor area. Bearing in mind that an average size of apartment in the development is circa 40m2, that one initiative has resulted in an additional £250,000 of GDV to the development.

Façade

The outer façade of the building can have a significant effect on the desirability of the property.

Many typical 1960/1970s office buildings appear devoid of character and aesthetic appeal, but the vast majority of the other core considerations are positive.

Amendments to the façade generally fall outside of current Permitted Development Rights. However planning permission to enhance the scheme by incorporating changes to the façade may well transform the look, feel and economic viability of the development.

I know of one commercial development which was an old BT telephone exchange and most certainly fell into the category of early 1960s tragic architectural design!

The developer very cleverly introduced additional windows and selective balconies for apartments, maximising natural lights and great views.

The unattractive external brickwork and bare exposed in-situ concrete frame structure had been given a thorough clean, localised repaired and then the exposed concrete frame painted a dark grey, matching the new window units and steelwork for the balconies. This gave the entire building a modern and sophisticated look and no doubt delivered a handsome return on investment, while regenerating an ageing building of yesteryear into a highly desirable building, providing homes for future generations.

Existing Floor Layouts

The existing layout of the building may have a marked impact on the number of units we can create in our residential development plans.

As a general rule of thumb we are looking at the overall gross floor area and dividing by 500 sq. ft. to get an initial guide of what potential the building may hold.

There are many factors that can affect this including:

• Size of floor plate: the floor plate dimensions will dictate whether we have a centre corridor with apartments running off either side or single apartments. Care should be taken on larger buildings, where the building runs deep and natural light may be difficult, to bring into the new residential apartments.

• Location of columns: The building will have been constructed with possibly office, retail or light industrial use in mind and hence its column placing, being an integral structural part of the building, may decide where we place major and minor internal walls to maximize the usable space within the building. Frequently the design will be replicable over the layout, i.e. the columns will have an even or predicable spacing, particularly on larger premises. However, this is not always the case so be sure to get your architect to check with a full measured survey to ascertain the unit density that can be achieved, floor by floor.

• Window openings: the line of the existing windows around the perimeter of the building will determine the shape and size of apartments, unless you wish to change the outside appearance and therefore planning will be required. Walls can be placed midway through windows, but this would need to be checked with the type of windows and the mullion design, otherwise modifications would need to be made.

- Slab to slab height: this is important to determine that there is sufficient headroom on each floor to allow for all necessary services, acoustic attenuation, ductwork for forced ventilation and extraction, fire suppression etc. Care should be taken to note down stand beam locations which will create pinch points with reduced headroom where the designers must navigate building services. Certain beams may not be able to take penetrations – precast concrete beams would be one example - so checks must be made. On multi-storey buildings it is likely that your upper apartments drainage will pass down through the slab and run under the soffit to the service shafts.

- Slab design load: The building must be able to take the imposed load of the intended design. In most of our examples, we are taking commercial premises and converting to residential where the design load will be much less. However, there may be consideration in older buildings where this may not be the case, hence another key task for your design team to determine.

Construction

The type of construction of the building will be of interest to your Structural Building Warranty provider and hence the success of your development. Checks should be made that the building has had no history of subsidence or any potential for future issues. Note close proximity of trees, watercourses and condition of existing drains. Also, look carefully for signs of older repairs to the building – mortar course repairs, cracks, distorted window and door frames etc.

The structure of the building could be:
- Traditional load bearing brick/blockwork
- Steel frame
- Precast concrete frame
- In-situ concrete frame
- Timber frame

- Modular construction
- Combination of the above

Certain types of construction, such as precast concrete slabs and facades, can create difficulties in the design and engineering process as well as being difficult to finance, so be aware of what the building construction is, ensuring that funders and warranty providers are satisfied.

The precast concrete slab process, for example, involves reinforcement bars which are an integral part of the design and

"ensuring that funders and warranty providers are satisfied"

will seriously limit your ability to insert apertures/penetration for services. Your structural engineer would be able to offer the advice required to assess what measures, such as trimming details, could be introduced to enable strategic services penetrations to be added.

Windows

The windows may be a high-cost item in your schedule of works. Office windows will probably have seen significant wear and tear and given their age, may require overhaul and refurbishment or replacement.

The compliance of the windows to meet modern-day building control requirements for thermal efficiency, means of emergency escape and locking mechanisms are crucial. Replacement windows may require planning, particularly if your development is in a conservation area, where very specific consideration will be given to the design and material type that will be allowed.

At first glance the windows may appear in good condition, but do bear in mind that the opening and locking requirements for office windows are very different to those of residential multi-storey dwellings. Consider children playing near open windows and the chill down the spine is enough to cement the need for your design team to make all the necessary allowances to achieve full building control compliance.

Should the decision be taken to change windows and to go through the planning process, then this is an ideal opportunity to take a step back and look at internal layout, window locations and mullion positions to ensure window locations are no longer a restriction on your optimal design.

Parking

What are the requirements for your demographic of clients with regards to parking? Your property may be inner city or village location, hence the design of your development would need to cater for your strategy.

Equally, planners and in particular the Highways department, will have a set of metrics to calculate exactly what parking your development will require.

One of the significant advantages of Permitted Development Rights is that parking is not generally considered in the application. One of our developments, which has permitted development rights for 26 apartments and 2 retail units, has just 8 parking spaces, whilst we have seen other developers' schemes have no parking provision directly on the development, relying on location of public services, local permit parking and cycling amenities including bike racks.

Utility services

Does the building currently have gas, water and electricity and if so at what capacity? A recent EquaGroup development had a very substantial electricity incoming supply but had no gas to the premises.

We had to decide whether the design should be to adopt an all-electric scheme or could we justify the cost of bringing in a new gas supply? If the scheme went all-electric, would the capacity be sufficient to satisfy the increased load or would we have to apply for additional capacity and potential upgrade of the local substation, at the developments cost? All are factors for your design team to consider in conjunction with very specific liaison with your gas and electricity providers.

One point to note on utility provider's quotes - the quotes are

"commercial properties often have commercial scale utilities"

only valid for a certain period of time and unless any reservation fee is paid, any capacity in the network is based on a first come, first served basis generally.

You could have a situation where you gain a quote, design your services and your economics around the quote, but by the time you have acquired the property and get to place the order, competitors or other development schemes in the local area, have used up the capacity and the quote would need to be re-issued and almost certainly at a higher cost to you.

As a basic reminder, do make sure that you take a note of all meter readings and cancel supply contracts on the day of acquisition, if required.

Equally, note that commercial properties often have commercial scale utilities that may still charge significant standing charges even if supply has ceased. This will need a very specific request to your supplier and possibly the services being capped to remove expensive standing charges that could run into thousands of pounds per annum.

Asbestos

The buildings we are selecting for consideration will be many years old. Historical building practices incorporated asbestos in many aspects of the building including:

Inside

1. Sprayed coatings on ceilings, walls, beams and columns
2. Asbestos cement water tank
3. Loose fill insulation
4. Lagging on boilers and pipes
5. AIB ceiling tiles
6. Toilet seat and cistern
7. AIB partition walls

8. AIB panels in fire doors

9. Asbestos rope seals, gaskets and paper

10. Vinyl floor tiles

11. AIB around boilers

12. Textiles e.g. fire blankets

13. Textured decorating coatings on walls and ceilings e.g. artex

Outside

14. Asbestos cement roof

15. Asbestos cement panels

16. Asbestos cement gutters and downpipes

17. Soffits – AIB or asbestos cement

18. Asbestos cement flue

Note: AIB - Asbestos Insulating Board

The duty to manage asbestos is contained in regulation 4 of the Control of Asbestos Regulations 2012. It requires the person who has the duty (i.e. the 'duty holder') to:

- Take reasonable steps to find out if there are materials containing asbestos in non-domestic premises and if so, its amount, where it is and what condition it is in.

- Presume materials contain asbestos unless there is strong evidence that they do not.

- Make and keep up-to-date a record of the location and condition of the asbestos-containing materials - or materials which are presumed to contain asbestos.

- Assess the risk of anyone being exposed to fibres from the materials identified.

- Prepare a plan that sets out in detail how the risks from these materials will be managed.

- Take the necessary steps to put the plan into action.

- Periodically review and monitor the plan and the arrangements to act on it so that the plan remains relevant and up-to-date.

- Provide information on the location and condition of the materials to anyone who is liable to work on, or disturb them.

There is also a requirement on others to co-operate as far as is necessary to allow the duty holder to comply with the above requirements.

How do duty holders comply with The Control of Asbestos Regulations 2012? There are four essential steps:

1. Find out whether the premises contain asbestos and if so, where it is and what condition it is in. If in doubt, materials must be presumed to contain asbestos.

2. Assess the risk from asbestos present in the premises.

3. Make a plan to manage that risk and act on it.

4. Provide this information to other employers (e.g. building contractors) who are likely to disturb any asbestos present, so that they can put in place appropriate control while the work is being done.

Source http://www.hse.gov.uk/asbestos/building.htm

While there is a legal requirement for a building owner to hold an Asbestos Register and something you should be requesting very early in the process, it is still surprising how many building owners cannot produce one.

"a legal requirement for a building owner to hold an Asbestos Register"

Your understanding of the risk of asbestos in the building, the implications of its management, its safe isolation and removal is ideally something you should be incorporating into your negotiation and offer on purchase price of the building.

This would be something we would regularly be discussing on each commercial property opportunity with the commercial agents from the start, to maximise the knowledge of the building and its potential for asbestos.

Foundations

While at first glance this might seem a strange inclusion when initially assessing the commercial property you are considering, it has been our experience over many years that numerous uncertainties can arise. Therefore the more information you can accumulate early in the process, the smoother the path of travel will be as you move through the various stages of your developments.

A recent development in Colchester was a case in point which caused us significant issues of time and cost, eating up a proportion of contingency which could otherwise have dropped to the bottom line at the end of the development, as profit.

Most developments would expect the ground floor concrete slab to be constructed of lightweight anti-crack mesh top and bottom and therefore there would be no issues in saw cutting drainage slots and manhole locations.

In this particular case, in the ground floor slab, we encountered a large-scale reinforced structural raft foundation which prohibited us from cutting to any depth, for fear of damaging the structural integrity of the foundation.

As-built drawings were requested for the building and were unavailable and as the building was not located in a flood area or in heavy clay, where ground heave might be considered an issue, we and our design team were, and still are, at a loss as to why this slab design was incorporated.

The engineered solution was to remove about 75mm of concrete cover locally on drainage runs, which was the maximum we could go without cutting the reinforcement. We then placed a 225mm raised floor across the entire ground floor of the building to enable sufficient fall for all drainage runs, rather than incorporating any pumped systems which were not favoured.

The moral of the story is that sometimes you simply cannot eradicate every risk in any walk of life and a development is a case in point. That is why we have important built-in contingency in terms of time and cost in numerous area of the development plan.

Condition

The overall condition of the building should be considered. However, one must undertake this in context with your intended design and refurbishment and therefore the visual appearance, or indeed imbedded issues in the property's current use, may not have a huge bearing on your future plans for that building.

The condition of the property might be broken down into a number of categories:

- Poor aesthetic condition – purely cosmetic and easily rectified in scope of works.
- Very poor aesthetic condition – requires some additional cost budget and time allowance.
- Structural – can be addressed with additional cost budget and time allowance.
- Major structural – very significant issues that may affect the viability of the scheme, or the building, in its current form.
- Ground issues - requiring remedial action with additional cost budget and time allowance.
- Serious ground issues – requiring partial or entire demolition.

It is always good practice to have any property you are considering buying, professionally surveyed – be that a RICS Red Book Valuation, Structural Survey or Building Survey etc.

So to summarise, your FIVE major considerations on the overall condition of the building may consider the following factors:

1. What are your design intentions?
2. What cost allowances have you made?
3. What time allowances have you made?
4. What permissions will you require?
5. What contingency have you allowed for?

Finding Your Site

Finding your site is probably one of the most frequent challenges and areas of angst for many property developers. In many ways it is a mind-set rather than an actual scarcity and with the right approach, systematisation, and focus on relationships that are built and seasoned over a period of time, the finding of your potential development project is not the hurdle many feel it is. There are a number of simple systems to follow as part of your systematic approach.

Property opportunities generally come from one of two main areas:

a. On market, i.e. they are currently being marketed out on social media and through agents.
b. Off market.

Let us take them one at a time.

On market

If a property is on market you must bear in mind that this is a formal process and this process has been triggered by the vendor under certain terms. We now have a third party involved in the process, which is the party who is marketing and has the responsibility to sell the unit. Areas to seek these kind of opportunities will include:

• Commercial agents

- Rightmove
- Zoopla
- Estates Gazette
- Estate agents
- Fleurets
- Daltons
- Auction
- Sourcing agents

When reviewing on market deals always check the accuracy of the details, where they are posted and how. Frequently there can be misclassifications and error in data.

It is your responsibility and yours alone to check the data and the information that is provided. This could include the usual information of address, EPC rating, square meterage, net internal area, gross internal area and local area. All of this information should form part of your detailed due diligence process.

Auction companies can be a great source of securing property relatively quickly. The auction process is not for the naïve. However with research and due diligence, ahead of time, some great opportunities can arise. Also note that offers can be made pre-auction and post-auction for lots that do not sell.

Some of the UK's main auction companies for commercial property include:

- Savills
- Barnard Marcus
- Allsop
- Auction House
- John Pye
- Countrywide Property Auction
- Pugh Auctions
- Edward Mellor
- Lambert Smith Hampton

- SDL Auctions

A great resource is www.eigpropertyauctions.co.uk who are very useful in searching for your requirements across the nationwide spectrum of auction companies.

You will have to pre-register for bidding at auction and bear in mind that the moment you have successfully bid on a property and the gavel goes down, you have technically exchanged contracts and must provide a deposit that day.

Some buildings may be listed on general websites, their own individual websites or through alternative sources. Keep an eye out locally in your area too. Central and local government may decide to sell their portfolio directly or via an agent, so relationships with local government departments can also indicate buildings that are on market.

Off market

This area is becoming increasingly more interesting. To identify opportunities that are not on market quite often **"savour and nurture the art of negotiation"** means there is reduced, if any, competition, which is encouraging. There is quite often a direct discussion between yourself and the owner of the property. There are no third party expectations to manage - direct conversation is an ideal opportunity to understand what great looks like to the vendor and try and shape a deal which works for both parties as a win-win. Remaining on this point - if you can savour and nurture the art of negotiation where you ask open questions and listen, truly understand and walk a mile in another party's shoes to understand how a deal can be shaped that works for them - if they are enthusiastic and prepared to commit their resources to close the sale, then this a great part of collaboration in the property investment and development sector.

Many parties steam into potential opportunities with a sense of entitlement and bravado. You must always bear in mind that the vendor, while possibly being a limited company or an LLP, also has a person or board behind them, be that a director or an officer of the company who will be making the decisions. I would encourage you to always table your offers formally and professionally but support your offers with authenticity, personal contact and commitment. Always be direct and transparent - I find this pays dividends in the long run and will be a great return on investment for you.

Finding off market opportunities

Where can we find off market opportunities? Well here is a list which will be helpful to you:

1. Private contacts: Let people know what you do. You will find many people will own or know of commercial properties and you want to be the first to know. People are interested generally in what you do, so private contacts are a core area.

2. Vendors: This can also include current owners of properties, or past owners of properties. If you have done a deal before, then it's likely that the building owner may well have other properties or know somebody who does own those properties. Stay close to your vendors, they are a great source of additional knowledge for further opportunities.

3. Sourcing agents: sourcing agents might be another source of further opportunity. Do be aware that you may well not be the only one that the sourcing agent has targeted with their off market deals, so caution should be extended. I would always encourage you to do your own due diligence as a sourcing agent will not provide any guarantees as to the information or due diligence that has been provided, so please be cautious in this area as indeed with all other areas.

4. Word of mouth: As mentioned earlier, private contacts are incredibly important so let people know what you do all the time. Use your own website, create attraction through social media with great content – this might include WhatsApp groups, Facebook, Twitter, Instagram, YouTube and LinkedIn. We have secured a £5m GDV development purely by this method.

5. The drive-by: It is always worth knowing your local area very well. Whenever you are in the area, drive by, make a specific point of looking at plans, maps, targeting areas or walking. Always have your eyes peeled and educate your close inner circle to do the same and capture opportunity. Remember Nigel's haircut!!

6. Publicly Available Tools: Use the tools that are available to all of us. That might include land registry, so you can have a look at local plans and local maps. Also use your due diligence - use land registry and do the searches, it's only about £3. Find out who owns certain properties. Have the conversations, contact the owners and you can also ask them about other opportunities they may have. Remember in Article 4 areas, all HMO landlords are on a register and you can go onto your local authority website and generally download which HMO owners have HMOs in that Article 4 area. This can be a great source of contacting your HMO landlords who may well have interests in commercial areas - you could contact them, asking if they have potential commercial buildings.

7. Specialist software: Specially designed software that draws on and aggregates market data from many independent sources can assist the prolific acquirer of commercial property. These are continuously updated and are generally available on a licensed subscription model.

8. Your professional team: Your professional team constantly work in this area, whether that be your structural engineer, architect or planning consultant etc. Build relationships with these professional teams, they are enduring and they will serve you well in the future. Any additional opportunity of new projects with a great relationship may well prove to create a strong return for both parties. With off market opportunities, as well as on market opportunities, speed and agility are everything.

9. Market movement: When looking at your local area and drive-by, look for movement in the market. It may be companies moving in or moving out or it may be buildings that are neither on the market nor off the market. These properties may have been vacant for some time. Keep your ears peeled about tenants moving, commercial leases moving or close to expiring or properties to let rather than to sell. All these are indications that there could be some movement.

10. Commercial agents: Commercial agents will be one of your core relationships in this sector.

Commercial Agents

The commercial agents know the market exceptionally well. They are extremely professional and very knowledgeable about the process. They have seen most approaches, are very familiar with how the negotiation process works, know the history of building purchases and are generally open to many different options of engagement. They require a close relationship, a clear understanding of your position, knowledge and understanding of your past track record. We prefer to be transparent about our intentions. The commercial agent is a business. It has, generally, a fixed overhead and its model is a success-based fee income on the successful exchange and completion of commercial premises and commercial properties.

Once you understand that, it will be very clear that the commercial agent is looking to back the party who they believe, in conjunction with the vendor, will deliver the most assured route to the property acquisition being completed. The worst scenario for a commercial agent is that the potential property purchaser takes the building right up the aisle and then ditches the building at the altar, so to speak! Your credibility, funding structure and the detailed language used in your offer is incredibly important in nurturing those relationships. Commercial agents have seen every type of individual walk through their door and they will want to screen you carefully, so spend quality time with your commercial agents to build that rapport.

How might an agent appraise you during your conversations? I believe there are four compelling elements that may have a significant bearing on your credibility in those first few discussions:

1. Your ability to complete – do you have the experience, tenacity, funding and guile to complete on a development that you may offer on?

2. One-off or a relationship – are you clear about whether you are just looking for a property or more interested in cultivating a long-term relationship?

3. Will you be able to create a sustainable income stream (or streams) over time? Our strategies within the EquaGroup of companies enable fees, directly or indirectly, for our commercial agent partners in the following areas:

   a. Fee on purchase of the commercial property

   b. Retainer fees for wider market search

   c. Sale of apartments in the development

   d. Fee on purchase of commercial units

   e. Fee for delivering commercial leases

   f. Managing commercial units annually over term

   g. Support in identifying opportunities in the future

   h. Creating Shared Value

4. Do we exude the qualities and integrity of Creating Shared Value?

"your return on time employed should be one of your highest profile KPIs"

If we were to calculate the fee income for a commercial agent from a single development purchase to that of a multiple development and ongoing and revolving relationship, across all our interests, then the fee comparison would be exponential!

It could be the difference between £10,000 and £250,000+ over many years – a compelling thought process, I think you would agree.

I would encourage you not to be competition focused, but rather have a sense of absolute clarity of what your company strategy is and not to compete with other parties' strategies.

As an example, we bid on an on-market opportunity which was looking at bids over £3m. It was a five story PDR scheme. Our bid went in at the £4.3 million mark, which was fine for the opportunity for our strategy. Another party secured the building at £5.5 million. Did they over pay for the development opportunity?

Well it depends. They were prepared to buy the building in cash, wait several years to go through full planning and appeal if necessary, to place three additional storeys on the building and develop a certain part of the car parking area. You cannot compete necessarily on that strategy if your strategy is just a permitted development strategy within the existing envelope of the building. So always be congruent to your strategy about what you are trying to achieve and decide if you want to take the time to bid on a property which may be saturated with many other investors. Remember your return on time employed should be one of your highest profile KPIs - after all, time is your most scarce resource.

When we are looking at commercial property, we are looking to force appreciation into the property, sometimes referred to as adding value. As you will see from the figure below, forcing appreciation has two key components:

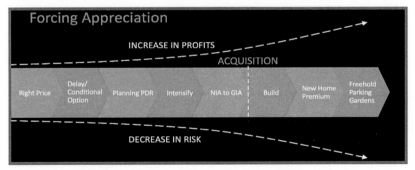

- The type of appreciation that is being forced in
- The timing of the appreciation being forced in

It is also worth considering the level of appreciation and in whose view.

Let me explain. You may view appreciation in your own terms, however it is often the funders' view of appreciation and that of your valuer's view that is equally important. We will discuss the valuer's view of appreciation a little later on in this book.

Let us take one step at a time on how we might force appreciation and when, into your property and the impact this can have on your risk and reward profile. Just some of the areas where we can force appreciation into our potential property purchase include:

1. Securing the property at the right price. The right price for us that is and in a win-win relationship with the vendor to cement the deal.
2. The conditionality of the offer and acceptance, which could include delayed completion, conditional exchange, or purchase option.
3. Planning and permitted development and the timing that it is secured.
4. Taking an existing planning and/or permitted development and intensifying it with revised permission, ideally within the timescale of the exchange.
5. Improving the area utilised from the existing net internal area to the larger gross internal area.
6. Building out the scheme by actually undertaking the refurbishment or construction.
7. Selling new homes by title splitting which can create a new home premium.
8. Sale of freehold parking, gardens and storage areas etc.

The first five of these can, in all likelihood be achieved prior to acquisition. Our skill and tenacity as a developer is to structure our offers, the conditionality and terms of that offer to secure the property acquisition on a win-win basis and to establish as many of those first five opportunities as possible, prior to acquisition. If we can achieve this, there is a strong potential that our commercial funders will value some enhancement accordingly and advance more leverage to the development. In certain cases it is possible to create additional forced appreciation and to bring them earlier, possibly forward prior to acquisition, but these tend to be on a much rarer basis.

Health and Safety

I have witnessed suffering to mankind that I would not wish others to experience. We all expect each other to come home safely to loved ones at the end of each day and a few points of common sense, self-awareness and consideration of our actions to others, goes a long way to ensure this happens.

It is important whilst finding property, to consider health and safety from the earliest point when you will almost certainly be conducting site visits. Be aware that site visits can be hazardous, even if these are not in a construction area. Please take suitable care and attention and form your own risk assessment prior to any visit. Be prepared and always have available your personal protective equipment including safety boots, hard hat, high visibility vest, gloves, eye protection and use your risk assessment to understand what is the best route and protection required.

Always remember that your first line of defence in health and safety will be

"consider health and safety from the earliest point"

your own common sense and reading the situation that you're about to step into. Always make sure that you are responsible for yourself and also assume responsibility for others, ensuring their access and actions on site are safe. Particularly be careful when accessing roof spaces, loft access, ladders and any areas at height. Many of the properties you will visit will be in a distressed condition - be aware these could possibly have been used by uninvited guests and may include unhygienic situations and potentially, drug paraphernalia. Always report unsafe acts or conditions to the agent or property vendor.

Occasionally you may be visiting construction sites and certainly you will be if your development moves to the next stage. During your assessment of principal contractors, you may well be visiting their current sites as part of your due diligence.

Irrespective of whether you are visiting your own construction site or another development, you will be expected to attend the site induction. This is a great opportunity

"The terms of your offer are vital and can set the tone of the development's risk profile"

for due diligence when you can check your principal contractor's case study sites during your due diligence phase of contractor selection. Make sure they abide by the rules on other developer's sites - be mindful whether the safety practices and culture on the site is something you would welcome on your development.

Ensure you know and follow all the regulations; the Health and Safety Executive (HSE) has a lot of very good quality guidance on their website. I recommend that you go to this website.

From a business perspective you must ensure you have these things in place in considering health and safety:

- Health and safety policy
- Health and safety statement
- Correct equipment
- Sufficient expertise and resource
- Training
- First Aid book
- Method statements
- Risk assessments
- Responsible person

The Health & Safety Executive is a great place to understand your duties and how to fulfil them, visit www.hse.gov.uk.

As with every other element of due diligence in your business, evaluate the expertise and knowledge available and consider engaging a professional to support you formally in this area to ensure compliance.

Making your offer

The terms of your offer are vital and can set the tone of the development's risk profile. Your vendor and/or commercial agent will have taken note beforehand of your professionalism, your openness, your explanation and your level of due diligence. They understand that the target is not to get to an offer; the target is to get to exchange of contracts effectively with a party who has the credibility and capability to do so.

The terms of your offer will need to be professionally presented and clearly understood by the commercial agent. It will include areas such as:

1. Property details you are offering on
2. Your offer price
3. The legal entity that is making the offer
4. The legal entity that will acquire the property – possibly a brand new SPV yet to be established, which is very common
5. Description of funding
6. Details of your solicitor
7. Any conditionality on VAT
8. List any other conditionality e.g. planning, timescales etc

Capital allowances have been available for many years, however to many this is an emerging strategy. Capital allowances could indeed form part of your due diligence. However, we find that they are generally not best figured into your due diligence and structuring of an offer, mainly because they are not assured in most cases until after you have secured control of the property and therefore not something that we build into our economic model at the time of offer.

It will take a period of time, cooperation and collaboration between your solicitor, capital allowances surveyor, accountant and the vendor to understand whether capital allowances have previously been claimed and whether you may take advantage of this tax benefit. Your surveyor will be able to work with your solicitor to ensure the correct clauses are placed in the exchange contract to enable capital allowances to be further explored in detail, post exchange of contracts.

Pause for thought - It's a people thing

Entering into a business relationship with someone is always an exciting time, with new opportunities and a learning process to go through.

Make sure you get that new relationship underway by following a few simple steps:

- Your gut feeling - do you like them? Are you comfortable telling others about the relationship? Is something just not stacking up? These are hugely important factors - do not leave anything unaddressed.

- Basic due diligence - The basic stages of due diligence in what you are going to do together.

- Extended due diligence - The detailed steps of understanding who you are going to be doing it with! Is honesty, integrity and rack record all 'as advertised'. Criminal record and directorship track record transparency - if you don't find out now, the banks will find out when you try to borrow as directors. Be open and most things can be discussed through.

- Values - does your future partner(s) share the same value ecosystem or at least are the values on a similar moral compass bearing to yours?

- Listen - do they listen to your views? So much trust or lack thereof, emanates from lack of respect through not listening

- Footprint - Remember that whatever you do, however you say it and what you produce generally leaves an audit trail that can not be extinguished. This goes for Companies House, social media and the web in general. Make sure each step passes muster very carefully, it will be time well spent.

- Openness - 'An open hand has the tightest grip'. Are you and your potential partner naturally being open and transparent with each other? Is there a feeling of 'should I show them this?' or 'why am I not being shown this?' If so larger issues may be at play.

Warren Buffett has a great phrase 'It is only when the tide goes out that you realise who has been swimming naked.' Don't wait for something to go off the rails before you act, or to realise what you could have known at the start with a little extra thought. Marketing can smooth over many cracks - make sure you understand this and go into new ventures with your eyes very wide open.

As a corporate trouble-shooter for several decades, I know how difficult it can be for some people to ask the tough questions in the good times. However, I can assure you that is much easier than having to unravel a disjointed or failed joint venture.

Be safe in entering JVs by using these simple steps and start your relationship on solid bedrock - ignore them at your peril.

4. Due Diligence

The greater danger for most of us lies not in setting our aim too high and falling short, but in setting our aim too low, and achieving our mark - Michelangelo

The due diligence phase is, without doubt, the most crucial phase of our 12-step fundamental system and indeed is integral to each and every fundamental. Time is of the essence. As time progresses so will your exposure, your costs and the amount of time you invest will increase, therefore it is important to ensure you get the fundamental decision-making criteria correct. That can only be achieved by ensuring that the level of your due diligence is thorough, robust and you are mindful of all risks, right from the offset, in evaluating your potential deal that has arisen. Create a systemised process that becomes your 'checklist' of areas to consistently evaluate and consider when doing your due diligence on a new commercial conversion or development opportunity.

Like all good systems they grow over time, becoming more comprehensive. Your due diligence system will be the same. View it as the backbone of your business, evolving it through tweaks and revisions each time new learning, situations and approaches are experienced. This way you will minimise the chances of repeating the same mistakes and will fine tune and optimise your assessing capability. At the time of writing this book, our development analysis tool is in the 26th revision showing how it is an integral part of recording our evolution.

A number of common errors can occur for the unwary when encountering development analysers:

1. Non-systemised approach to due diligence. This can lead to certain layers of analysis being missed out completely.
2. Deal analysers using basic Excel spreadsheets that are incomplete, inaccurate and non audit checked.
3. Core data not taken from reliable sources
4. No sensitivity analysis
5. Costs not fully identified
6. No cash flow modelling

When you do your due diligence, anything you fail to identify at this stage, which later emerges and impacts your decision-making process, could be extremely expensive. In terms of return on investment, proper structured investment at the start of your process will ensure that your evaluation criteria are formed on solid bedrock, not on shifting sand.

We have invested heavily in creating a nationally-renowned development analysis tool. We refer to our due diligence as bank grade due diligence and quite rightly so, given the fundamental reliance of any commercial conversion and development is on the utilisation of leverage from commercial funders. Therefore, our due diligence must stand the rigours and robust testing and evaluation of our funders, credit risk department and their policies.

Bank grade due diligence is crucial to understanding how each one of our stakeholders will evaluate, whether that be our commercial funding partners, private investors, valuers and many of the other areas we will look at later on in the process. Once you have systemised your due diligence it will become a relatively swift process to get the core data and initial assessment undertaken. You may eventually be able to get your initial due diligence concluded within a matter of hours, however as you start your journey in evaluating developments, this may well take several days. However, with a systemised approach, you will be able to improve on this substantially.

Development Analyser

A development analyser is, generally, an Excel spreadsheet which encapsulates all your initial due diligence into one file, enabling you to identify the core factors to draw conclusions as to what your next decisions need to be.

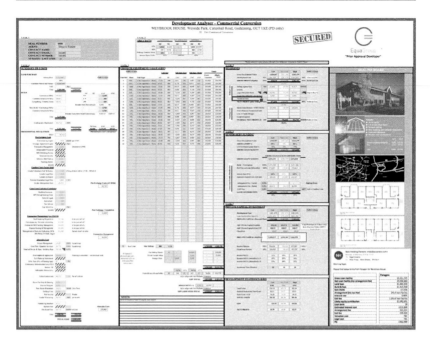

Frequently the land purchase price is the first element that draws one's eye when looking at a development opportunity. The reality is that it is one of the FINAL conclusions we are driving towards, hence the culmination of all of our due diligence and analysing will come down to what is the best offer price we can make on the property, for our given strategy.

The equation is:

GDV – All Development Costs – Developer Profit = Maximum Purchase Price

There are 14 core areas to a development analyser – each part of which can have multiple sub-sections. This does not necessarily mean that it takes an age to undertake. With practice, the due diligence of the first deal lasting 1-3 days can be quickly shortened to just a few hours.

What are the components within the development analyser? Well here is an overview of each, many of which will be covered in more detail in later chapters.

1. Gross Development Value

The GDV is where we calculate the likely end valuation of our finished product which generally will include leasehold sale of apartments, freehold sale, sale of gardens, car parking and storage areas.

2. Local comparable statistics

This is the base data from sold comparables of similar products in the area. For instance, if our product is a one bedroom apartment on a ground floor location of 40sqm then we would be searching for similar criteria within 0.5 km (ideally within the same postcode!) to determine past evidence of sold comparables.

3. Freehold Sale & Ancillary items

There is uncertainty in the market in this area with government intervention endeavouring to control the often historically found issues of unfair practices of indexation on ground rents well above that of inflation and retail price index levels. The other areas of valuation interest are car parking, storage units, any garaging, gardens and other ancillary areas of benefit.

4. Build/Refurbishment costs

This would be the anticipated refurbishment of the property based on existing and proposed floor areas with additional certainty being provided through our professional team.

5. Professional fees and other costs

a. Pre-exchange costs

This includes all costs that would be expended using seed capital prior to your development private capital being deployed. If the development failed to exchange contracts, then this would be the ultimate value of any abortive costs

b. Costs from exchange to completion

These are the costs that enable the development to progress to legal completion, after exchange of contracts. Given that you are now committed to purchasing this property after exchange of contracts, decisions can be made on the risks of taking planning/permitted development to the next stage, subject to conditionality, as well as seeking final utility quotes and progressing the detailed design etc.

c. Allowable/non-allowable costs

Your senior debt funder will fund certain 'allowable' costs and others costs they will not entertain. It is <u>important</u> for the developer to understand the correct terminology and which costs sit in which category, as this will affect cash flow and private investor funding levels required.

d. Transaction management

These are the costs and management time required to drive through the legal conveyancing, funding and private investor on-boarding as well as establishing the company secretarial aspects of formalising a new company.

e. Selling costs

The selling costs will include, but not limited to brochures, computer generated images (CGI), sales and marketing, estate agent's costs, legal fees for conveyancing (leasehold and freehold), title splitting and furnishing show apartments etc.

6. Contingency

Always apply a contingency within your numbers, typically somewhere between 5% and 20%, depending on your experience, the complexity of the scheme, the condition of the building and how many knowns and unknowns you have at this stage. Your contingency will be allocated in several areas including build costs, duration of development, funding, professional fees, cash flow and GDV.

7. Property area data

This will be the original base data of the property and your assessment of what can be undertaken through your particular planning strategy to create new homes. The base data must be accurate so conduct checks on the area/dimensions. Through an initial assessment of circa 45 – 50 sq.m (500sp.ft) per apartment, you will be able to make a very high level assessment on how many apartments might be designed into a property. If you find this difficult to assess initially always utilise a designer to support you.

8. Development returns and summary

With all the data you are processing you will need to assess how to pull the information together, to make sense of it and to make informed decisions. This will include your gross and net profit positions. You may include tax implications on your development model also although, due to complexity, this is often kept separate and all numbers discussed are net of tax.

9. Finance costs – senior debt, bridge mezzanine etc

Cost of funds usually ranks 3rd in magnitude after purchase price and refurbishment costs, hence this needs careful thought on your chosen strategy. This analysis would be supported by a draft term sheet from your broker typically, who would be able to turn this around within 24-48 hours.

10. Private capital

Private investors will be your source of capital through a variety of channels. What the development analyser should show you very clearly is what amount of private capital you require for this development.

11. Development Statistics

Establishing trends in your systems is important and the more analysis you undertake, the more valuable trends you will see and the more confident your language will be when discussing developments with funders, private investors and commercial agents. Key performance indications (KPIs) and data for internal analysis, hurdle rate assessment and risk evaluation will often come from this source and will help you to assess your forecast performance v actual and aide continuous improvement.

12. Cash flow

Cash flow is frequently missed from many development analysers I have seen, however it remains a fundamental element. Your cash flow will affect the amount you are asking your private investors for and hence getting an accurate range of private investor capital early is essential to avoid any corrections later.

13. Sensitivity Analysis

An important part of risk management is sensitivity analysis in understanding what happens if two or more variables move in different directions. If GDV reduces we have a problem; if build costs increase we have a bigger problem; if build duration increases as well then we have extended funding costs as well so we would be

"simulating the due diligence of the red book valuation"

experiencing exponential economic downward pressures. Likewise, if GDV increases, the build came in under budget and most of the contingency remains unspent, the profit will increase.

14. Land Purchase

Finally, once all the other elements have been analysed we use our equation: GDV – All Development Costs – Developer's Profit = Maximum Purchase Price to ascertain the maximum price we are prepared to offer on the property purchase.

Our comparables will be taken from historic prices only and we must understand how the sale price relates to the actual unit that has been sold in the past. We achieve that by using the national EPC Register (www.epcregister.com) to identify the sales unit rate (sq m & sq ft) of the house or apartment that has been sold. We then apply that as an average of those examples in the local area, within as tight as possible proximity – ideally a 0.25-0.5 km radius maximum.

Ensure that you look at the sensitivity of whether we are in a rising market or a falling market. How far in the past was each comparable sold? The presumption is that property price increase over time, however the time scale of our due diligence is over a short period of time and we must understand where we are in the property cycle.

We will also evaluate potential sales with the local agents and their aspiring view as to what those units, once created in 9-24 months, might realise in sales.

We will also look at a RICS Red Book Valuation. However, by the time you see this report you will have paid £3,000 - £6,000 hence it is best to anticipate its content by simulating the due diligence of the Red Book Valuation Survey will undertake!

We may have evidence of other developments that we or others have done in the local area, so we may have access to other information to help us verify with greater accuracy the GDV.

In addition to the leasehold sales we will examine the proceeds from the freehold sale, once we have title split, assuming this is a buy, develop and sell strategy. This will be covered in a later chapter in detail.

Other areas where we may be able to create additional value is the sale of any car parking spaces, etc, and any ancillary spaces, such as garages, storage areas and gardens.

This due diligence will support our GDV assessment which will later be verified by the Red Book Valuation. Once we have achieved the potential Gross Development Value plus the Gross Development Costs, we can then look at the cost of funding. The cost of funding will be from the senior debt provider through your broker. We will then get a draft term sheet, which generally takes between 24 - 48 hours to produce from our commercial broker, hence it is important to work quickly and anticipate the strength and depth of the professional team you will require.

Your funding structure should also be understood at the very early stages, whether you are applying senior debt, private investment loans, your own capital and therefore, your own cost of capital or any mezzanine funding etc. All of those costs should be evaluated in the initial assessment. There will also be costs to sell, should your strategy be to title split and sell or to sell as a non-title split unit. That strategy would include any necessary selling and legal and splitting fees, which also need to be included. Your overall summary of numbers will give you your initial assessment of your gross profit and also your overall net profit, post funding costs.

It is important to understand the economics of the project, in the eyes of our joint venture partner. Should a joint venture partner be bringing in capital for a shareholding/profit share return of the business, then it would be sensible to provide a set of numbers which establishes the potential capital required and what the shareholding and returns would be. We simulate the return on capital employed over time, to establish with the joint venture partner what their returns are likely to be.

We will also assess the term that is required for this development. That programme is important for the return on investment calculations. This will include time to get to:

- Exchange of contract
- Legal completion
- Design and tendering
- Construction/refurbishment
- Selling, including conveyancing of apartments
- Paying bank senior debt back
- Paying investor capital back
- Orderly closing of SPV
- Returning shareholders proportion of net profits

As a business investor I have seen many cases where investment memorandums fail to recognise all of these programme implications and potentially leave private investor expectations unmet, if indeed the development raises its funding in the first place!

> **"Good business practice anticipates change with sensitivity analysis helping you stress test your economic model"**

There are a lot of variables in the due diligence process, many of which do not have to be created from scratch. For instance, your legal fees may not vary too much, from transaction to transaction and certainly, initially, an estimated number will be more than adequate. Some solicitors will work on a % per each £m of purchase price. Our ability to do this due diligence quickly can improve very rapidly with time.

Sensitivity Analysis

Good business practice anticipates change with sensitivity analysis helping you stress test your economic model to ensure that it is robust enough to absorb challenges that may occur in the future.

Understanding the variables on your development will help you assess each and every moving part and the forces that can be applied to them – internally and externally.

Rather than looking one dimensionally we must assess risk in a multi-dimensional way.

There are risks that any variable may change and some of the prominent areas that require continuous assessment include:

- GDV value
- Cost of refurbishment
- Refurbishment programme
- Senior debt terms
- Programme for senior debt
- Valuation process
- Freehold sale
- Cash flow

Remember that each of these can change up or down thus applying a positive or negative effect. The challenge is to ensure that you move the variables in a favourable direction on a compounded basis, but let us consider if this works in a compounding negative way.

Example 1: Negative effect

Situation: GDV reduces by 5%, build costs increase 5%, build programme increases by 2 months, funding costs increase by 2 months of interest.

Financial effect: Costs increase, revenue reduces, profit reduces, risk increases

.

Example 2: Positive Effect

Situation: GDV increase by 3%, build costs are on-budget with no contingency spent, build programme on target with no contingency utilised, funding costs on budget with no contingency used.

Financial effect: Costs on budget, contingency released to bottom line, revenue increases, profit increases, risk reduces.

Whilst these 2 examples are at very high level it should help you consider the compounded effect of how variables can move and the sensitivity effect it will have on your economic model.

Once you have run a sensitivity analysis on many of your variables, you will need to check whether the fundamentals of the project still survive intact. If they do not, you need to look at your risk and how you can mitigate, transfer and/or manage that risk.

Risk

The very essence of this book is about understanding the risk and reward profile you may choose to take and the considerations that you will take on your journey of growth and control.

We are all different and our appetite for risk will vary. Having said that, as owners of a business we must understand the factors that have the potential to bring risk and the probability of that risk occurring.

The risk equation is:

Risk = Impact x Probability / Cost.

Impact is the effect on the business should a risk event occur.

Probability is the likelihood that the event might occur over a period of time. Cost is the financial cost it takes to mitigate or reduce the risk to an acceptable level.

Risk & reward evaluation is the decision making process that you will need, to find where opportunity may lie for you.

Produce a risk register on every one of your developments. Create a standard ranking on risks that are likely to be found. This becomes your risk checklist and then you are not starting from scratch on each development but building on the previous. This checklist will provide prompts on every one of your new developments. On your risk register, you will look at probability versus impact, you will look at the risk that resides before intervention, then, when identified, the measures you're taking to reduce risk and then the remaining risk that you are left with, after you have taken your risk reduction measures.

Once you have identified the risks, you can either:

- Mitigate risk
- Transfer risk
- Manage that risk

They are your three areas. Once you have gone through that process, you then monitor that risk consistently throughout the life of the project.

To best identify, assess and monitor risk, I suggest that you use and maintain a Risk Register for your business. Rolled up over time this will become an invaluable memoir and checklist for your business operations and a method for you to demonstrate risk management in action and measurement of your progress and success.

Columns which you may wish to include on your risk register include, but are not limited to:

- Risk description
- Ownership
- Risk rating (before Action Plan)
- Category
- Probability
- Impact
- Consequence
- Rating - typically RED/AMBER/GREEN
- Mitigation measure taken
- Risk rating (after Action Plan)
- Probability
- Impact

- Rating - typically RED/AMBER/GREEN
- Residual risk measurement
- Impact on cost
- Current status
- Status date action required

The list of potential risks can become quite considerable over time, so be sure to maintain vigilance and records with regard to the overall risk management process.

Some examples of development risks that would be worthy of consideration on your list:

- Down valuation on Senior Debt funding by RICS Redbook Valuation/Monitoring surveyor
- Failure to discharge planning conditions
- Compliance with CDM Regulations
- GDV impacted by market conditions
- Cash flow insufficient in SPV to fulfil obligations
- Main contractor tenders are over budget
- Design creep increases tender costs
- High level of variations from main contractor with time and cost impact
- Contingency levels dwindling and monitoring surveyor indicates to bank that injection of developer funds may be required to restore contingency levels.
- Delays in construction progress
- Delays in design
- Delays in planning approvals
- Health and safety incident
- Dispute with supply chain
- Reputational risk
- Disagreement with shareholders
- Neighbour boundary or party wall dispute
- Main contractor goes into administration

- Can not sell units in time to pay back senior debt within development term.
- Vendor pulls out at the 11th hour before exchange and seed capital is lost.
- Designer fails to perform, which impacts main contractor progress.

As we can see, some of these may be extreme and others less so. However somewhere, at some time, a development has experienced each one of these, sometimes multiple occurrences sadly. In my role as a global trouble-shooter in corporate life, when some of these incidents have happened, that would be when I would receive a call to 'parachute into a corporate war zone' and conduct a thorough investigation, collecting and wading through the evidence and establishing a turnaround programme if applicable.

This is an extremely unpleasant position for all parties and obviously a devastating position for the families and close colleagues in the event of a major health and safety incident. A strong level of proactive focus, diligence, awareness and discharge of responsibilities is best advised to avoid an 'after the event' reactive approach.

Professional Team

Your professional team is a critical part of your development and is an extension of you. They are your leverage.

You should consider investing a lot of time pre-qualifying your professional team, making sure they are right for you, that there is a right fit, they share your code of values and systems, they have the right skills and expertise that you will require on each one of your developments. Not every member of your professional team will be right for every development, as each development will have its own individual requirements. I would encourage you to invest time with your professional team and grow a relationship and a rapport. Your team will inevitably grow over time.

Look continuously at how you spread your work around with your professional team. If you have ten developments and place a contract with ten architects, you spread your risk, but, equally, you're not creating the rapport necessary. If you put all 10 developments with one architect, then, potentially, you are creating concentration risk within that relationship. So manage carefully how you grow your professional team, who you use and how you deploy them wisely.

Your professional team will be highly experienced and have the expertise to deal with certain requirements. Your role is to understand which areas of expertise you need, which areas of your professional team cover what and how you create that interlocking relationship between them. Ensure as much of the risk is mitigated as possible, most of the reward is extracted favourably for you and the compliance is assured within your development.

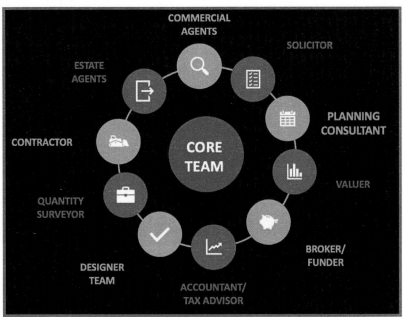

We like to ensure that our professional team embody our unofficial slogan as a business – 'well advised'. If you start off being well advised, you will have one of the incredibly important strengths of humility as a business person. Humility means that you will be able to access other people's knowledge willingly and gratefully and understand how they complement and enrich your business plan.

Who might be in your professional team? Well, there are any number of parties which may vary from development to development. These are probably your priority list:

- Commercial agent
- Solicitor
- Planning consultant
- Valuation surveyor
- Commercial broker
- Commercial funder
- Accountant
- Tax advisor
- Design team
- Quantity surveyor
- Main contractor
- Estate agent

Design Team

A key member of your professional team is your design team. This can be broken down into many different elements within your professional team. It will include:

- Architect
- Structural engineer
- Acoustic engineer
- CDM team
- Building services engineers
- Building control
- Fire specialists
- Building surveyor
- Ground investigation
- Environmental engineers
- Capital allowances surveyors

- Asbestos/refurbishment & demolition surveyor
- Party wall specialists
- Interior designer

Measurement

The standard of measurement in some property sales brochures and supporting information can have some variances to what is actually there!

Your due diligence should include a full survey to establish the facts, prior to making substantial headway into the conveyancing process and will often form one of the first duties of your design team.

The Royal Institute of Chartered Surveyors (RICS) whom we will hear more about in the Valuation chapter of this book, are the guiding authority for national and international standards of property measurement.

New standard forms of measurement and definitions are being introduced to standardise global measurement standards, however much of the traditional language of measurement still remains in mainstream use and these are:

- GEA: Gross External Area
- GIA: Gross Internal Area
- NIA: Net Internal Area

The new standards have started to be introduced from 2015 through the International Property Management Standards and their terminology is reasonably similar to the above definitions with a few notable examples.

The table below and the following summary provides a compare and contrast across the old and the newer incoming terms:

New Terminology	Old Terminology
IPMS 1	Equates closely to GEA (gross external area)
IPMS 2 - Office	Equates closely to GIA (gross internal area)
IPMS 3 - Office	Equates closely NIA (net internal area)
Internal Dominant Face	Internal face of the external wall

IPMS 1:

IPMS 1 is similar to the Gross External Area measurement and is measured externally.

What is included:

- Areas with headroom <1.5m
- Areas of internal partitions and walls
- Perimeter wall thickness
- Columns
- Stairwells
- Chimney breasts
- Lift-wells
- Garages
- Outbuildings with a party wall to main building

What is excluded:

- Covered corridors and pathways
- Balconies
- Fire escape
- Vehicle parking areas
- Roof terraces

Where is this usually used:

- Estimating building cost plans
- Planning applications and approvals
- Rating and council tax

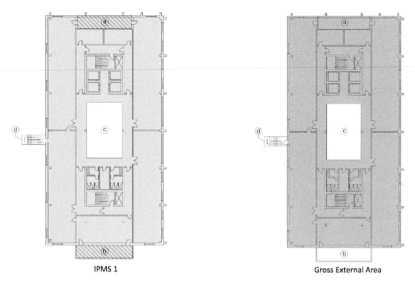

IPMS 1   Gross External Area

IPMS 2:

IPMS 2 is similar to the Gross Internal Area measurement.

It is measured to the internal face of the perimeter walls. The internal face is the brick/block work plus plaster coat - not the surface of internal linings installed by the occupier.

What is excluded:

- External projections
- Perimeter wall thickness
- Canopies
- External balconies

Where is this usually used:

- Estimating building cost plans
- Property management - service charge calculations
- Residential homes valuation
- Estate agency and valuations - marketing and valuation of warehouses and industrial buildings

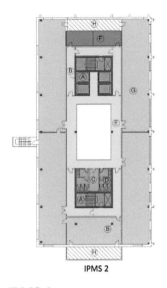

IPMS 2

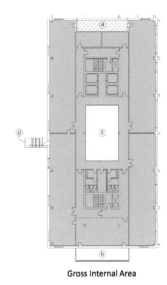

Gross Internal Area

IPMS 3

IPMS 3 is similar to the Net Internal Area measurement and is measured to the internal face of the perimeter walls.

What is excluded:

- Meter cupboards
- Lift lobbies, lift-wells and lift rooms
- All common parts:
- Entrance halls
- Landings and balconies
- Toilets
- Cleaners' rooms
- Corridors
- Plant rooms
- Fuel stores and tank rooms
- Stairwells
- Columns

- Chimney breasts

Where is this usually used:

- Estate agency and valuation - shops and offices
- Property management - service charge calculations

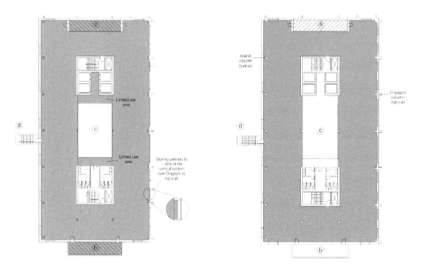

IPMS 3 Single Occupancy   Net Internal Area

For further information, refer to the International Property Management Standards at The Royal Institute of Chartered Surveyors

Source: https://www.rics.org/uk/

Build & Refurbishment Costs

During your due diligence phase, you will be pulling together a cost estimate of the likely build budget for your development. At this time, you will probably not have the design or the plans and probably not any tendering process either. To the new developer this can be an intimidating period. However there are a number of methods of assessing construction costs at this early stage:

- Ask your architect to produce a draft budget

- Employ a quantity surveyor or estimating company who will produce a broad cost plan
- Ask a 'friendly' main contractor to visit site and produce a cost plan
- Use your historical data of previous development completed
- Use unit budget rates similar to the tables below
- Possible joint venture

Before any of these however, you must be able to convey the intentions of the scheme in simple terms through a written brief. This can be as high level as a sketch of building layout however would ideally include:

- Measured floor plan of existing and proposed
- Clarity of your end product
- Type of construction method – new build or refurbishment etc.

For those that use imperial or metric it can be confusing to alternate between the two. A broad brush conversion for mental arithmetic is 10 sq. ft. = 1 sq. m however the actual conversion rate 10.764 sq. ft. = 1 sq. m

There are unlimited permutations of build, refurbishment, extension and structural build programmes that all have varying levels of complexity as well as a wide range of locational issues that will affect price, preliminaries, risk and deliveries etc.

For the purpose of this chapter we will be looking at high level unit rates (sq. m and sq, ft) applicable to two primary areas:

- Refurbishment for commercial conversions
- New build houses

Refurbishment for commercial conversions

There are many dependencies on pricing development refurbishment costs including:

- Location in the country
- Quality of finishes for your product

- Number of bedrooms
- Size of apartments
- Utilisation factor of GIA space
- Lifts
- Services – all electric v gas & electric
- Demolition
- Structural – underpinning etc
- Damp/tanking requirements
- Roof
- Windows
- Facade
- Foundations and structural
- Asbestos
- Balconies
- Temporary works & scaffolding requirements
- Utilities – existing v proposed
- Location with other buildings
- Site space for contractors materials, site cabins etc

Contingency dependent on:

- Stage of development
- Complexity
- Between 5-12% typically

Area	£ per sq meter	£ per sq ft
Apartments	£1,100 - 1,350	£ 100 - 125
Common Areas	£300 - 700	£27 - 65

New build houses

One of the primary differences between refurbishment and new build is ground works. The moment you open up the ground the risk levels increase. Whilst extensive surveys, soil investigation and ground radar etc can determine certain characteristics, there will always be other risks to which your contractor will be exposed to such as ground conditions, weather, obstructions, contamination etc and they will understand this and price the risk accordingly, or exclude from their tender.

Some of the additional consideration over and above the refurbishment risks mentioned previously include:

- Main frame type – steel frame, in-situ reinforced concrete (RC), precast concrete, brick & block and modular etc
- Number of storeys
- Planning requirements (including conservation)
- Ground remediation
- Ground conditions/foundations
- Estate roads
- Utility connections
- S106/CIL/AH requirements
- Specification

Contingency dependent on:

- Stage of development
- Ground risks
- Complexity
- Between 10-20% typically

Area	£ per sq meter	£ per sq ft
Houses	£1,550 - 1,900+	£ 145 - 175+

Pause for thought - Why we won't always get what we have always got!

Ever heard that quote? Well I did 20 years ago and have loved it until recently BUT now I do NOT believe it is true any longer.

Why?

Well, the world is moving at a meteoric rate, change is all around us. Whether that be with Artificial Intelligence, driverless cars, the end in sight of the 'mine and burn' hydrocarbon economy or with crypto-currencies emerging at a phenomenal rate, the changing face of online retailing or even the rapidly reducing concentration time levels that society has…..

If we fail to embrace change, we will fail to even stand still - we will become increasingly insignificant in this world!

The externalities are moving rapidly and we have a simple choice - change and adapt or fail to change and be subservient to those that do decide to change. That is how the major corporations with a future are thinking. They are not only meeting current demand, but also anticipating change and working out what will influence and serve future needs and problems.

There is no 'staying put' in life - you either change and evolve or don't change and degrade, withering on the vine. A simple choice really.

As entrepreneurs we strive and thrive each day to make the difference and build a better, more fulfilling life of wealth, in all its forms and enrich the lives of others around us.

It starts with mastery of our-self, our attitude, our approach, our desire and our first and ensuing steps that build a momentum of embracing change with a long term mind-set that will endure.

5. Planning

If I had eight hours to cut down a tree, I would spend six of them sharpening my axe -
Abraham Lincoln

Gaining planning is one of the most feared and misunderstood parts of property development. It is a complex and ever-changing environment and requires specialist support, from a planning consultant, to help you demystify the process.

Is your glass half full or half empty?

Well, your approach in life and your approach to planning can be seen in a similar vein.

Planning, the system and the process can either be something that:

- Agitates you, gets you all worked up, something out of control and the arch nemesis, or
- Custodians of society who enable the right decisions in the best interests of our community and with the right knowledge - something we as developers can work with, not against, to enable great opportunities.

Deciding what part planning permissions will play in forcing appreciation into your development will determine your 'risk adjusted reward' dimension in your deployment strategy.

Planning can be a complex and ever-changing environment and is certainly an area for the experts, which is why your planning consultant will be invaluable for you and should be one of the first engagements of your professional team.

Striking the right risk and reward balance for your property aspirations and business is one of the most important fundamentals that you must decide on quickly to avoid wasted effort, resource and time. A crucial component of this is deciding what your planning angle is. This may vary from having a strategy that:

- Avoids planning completely
- Protects against planning risk: conditionality of offer to purchase, subject to planning.
- Is prepared to take planning risk – if this is your strategy then it would be wise to build your base case upon not receiving planning for the optimum scheme and allowing a Plan B, fall-back position.

If seeking to protect yourself through conditionality on planning, do be aware that there may still be significant seed capital costs of applying for planning which should not be underestimated, such as architect fees, planning consultants fees and planning submission fees etc. As your relationship grows with your professional team you may find that they will be prepared to work on a partially or wholly contingent basis, in the early stages, which may help to reduce your exposure.

The funders have a very clear interest in your planning strategy. In simple terms, if you have not got planning then development finance will be extremely hard to get. You will probably be securing the property on a bridge with a valuation based on the property's current valuation and use – so this might be as a vacant retail unit for example.

The Planning Opportunity

I want to take you back to our earlier chapter where we discussed how forcing appreciating into our property asset is absolutely key. The degree to which we can do this, over and above the basis of the agreed purchase price of the build, will be a significant determinant on our profitability of the end conversion or development scheme.

The following property development angles illustrate the potential growth in risk adjusted returns:

Strategy	Planning Risk	Forced Appreciation
Residential flip	Very low	Low
Changes of use	Medium risk	Medium
Commerical Coversions- Permitted Development	Low/Medium	Medium
Commerical Coversion Permitted Development + Planning	Medium/High	Medium/High
Land new build - Planning + Development	High	High

Naturally these levels are generic and while there will be highly profitable flips and less profitable permitted development conversions, the illustration hopefully cements a clear reminder that planning has a direct relationship between quantum of risk and reward.

To ensure you have the right strategy for you, your goals and the resources available to you, deciding your planning approach is crucial before you start looking at specific buildings.

Planning Consultant

Once you have your business strategy and planning clear in your mind, then you will need to identify and engage with a great planning consultant who will be able to help you clarify your approach.

It is also helpful to have your planning consultant verify your search area. As an example, if you had decided that your two target areas were Bracknell in Berkshire and Alton in Hampshire and your strategy was commercial conversions under permitted development rights, then it might be helpful to understand that both of these areas have Article 4 restrictions applied to them by the local authorities which enables them to opt out of the permitted development rights for the area.

Your planning consultant will charge you however - you are running a business and every business has a cost base. Set your cash flows out, forecast your expenditure and then fund your start up enterprise accordingly. This will be money well invested.

Until you become very proficient at finding and offering on commercial property, use your planning consultant on properties that you are serious about. This will depend on your intentions and the planning consultant will want to understand exactly what you intend to do or what is in the 'art of the possible'. After years of successful transactions, we still use a planning consultant on most developments.

With planning there may well be a certain number of steps in the process which will better determine an outcome and your planning consultant will be best able to help you determine that roadmap, the fees and the time that it will take.

This is important if you are applying conditionality to your offer to the vendor, as the management of expectations on timescales must be considered from exchange of contracts to legal completion and the long stop date.

The Local Plan and serving society

The Planning Inspectorate supports the Government's aim for every area in England to have an adopted plan. A local plan sets out local planning policies and identifies how land is used, determining what will be built and where. Adopted plans provide the framework across England.

Source: www.gov.uk/guidance/local-plans

As developers it is important we are aware and understand the Local Plan, what it means to our strategic deployment of resources and in what areas to identify opportunity.

Developments of scale enable us to maximise leverage of the skills and experience of our professional team who will always have niche experience at a scale far greater than we can personally have. This is our advantage – we are the conductor of a very large orchestra and our role is to ensure we have each part of that orchestra engaged, at the right time, in concert with each other.

It will be these experts who will be able to best assess the direct and indirect implications of planning regulation and the Local Plan, for your strategy in your area.

Setting the planning context

Why do we need planning? A simple question but one which often gets missed.

Society in the UK does not have enough homes to meet demand. This is consistently monitored by Government and policy is continually adapted to stimulate additional homes deployed by national and local home builders. Permitted development and Help To Buy are two such examples of intervention.

So the demand is required and if most predictions are to be believed, this demand is not going to be satisfied anytime soon.

I know myself, living in Surrey and having four children that the opportunity for them to acquire their first property and get on the property ladder is not going to be easy, with even one bedroom apartments frequently costing £200k+.

That is why we are looking to educate our children differently to enable them to enter adulthood with many of the skills and plans in place, some significantly advanced enough for them to take advantage of the property market, rather than be subservient to it.

The planners must enable a careful balance between control of development, as custodians of our environment, as well as relaxing and controlling opportunities for these much-needed homes to be deployed in the most appropriate and responsible manner.

We, as developers, must take time to understand the rules defining planning, how they are likely to evolve and indeed how this change process materialises, to enable us to anticipate change and seize the opportunity.

"Society in the UK does not have enough homes to meet demand"

Your planning strategy

What is your approach to planning risk?

This lies right at the heart of your development strategy.

Are you prepared to take a punt and buy a property and then pump in thousands of pounds in trying to get planning over several years, hoping to goodness that you are successful? Well, a few do, however they may well have the resources to operate this strategy.

Most business decisions (and let us remind ourselves that as developers, that is what we are running - a business), are made by weighing up the risk, reward, resources, opportunity and making decisions on what to pursue and what not to.

Saying 'no' is a very important part of business!

Your funder will have a very active interest in your intentions and for the avoidance of doubt, the funder will only fund what they see and what you can evidence.

If you have a vacant commercial building, that is what they will value and loan a certain proportion against.

If you have a vacant commercial building with full planning permission for conversion to 20 apartments, they will now be able to offer commercial development funding options - but only once the planning is actually in place.

The roadmap you lay out is as much a fundamental part of your strategy as the end intention.

If your strategy is to hold residential units after your development completes, then the economic impact of that needs to be factored in.

Let me explain:

The funding of residential properties held in companies may be circa 70% LTGDV (Loan to Gross Development Value)

If you have an economic strategy for your development of say 15% net margin on GDV after funding costs, which is held in equity, then you will have to find the difference between what the market will fund and what you hold in equity, if you are to re-finance successfully.

So the implication that you will be considering, based on 'starting with the end in mind' include:

- Your model for investors in the development
- When will they exit with returns
- Profitability of your overall strategy of forcing appreciation
- Whether you hold or sell
- Funding levels of completed development
- Equity levels that exist, post investor payback, plus returns
- Other funds required, their timing and cost base

As is clear from the above chronology, it is essential that you understand what your end game looks like and build the strategy, ground up, to get to that end.

If you get this wrong and need to change your strategy midway through a development, it can get complicated with VAT, tax and funders, but not irretrievably so. Always take the best advice on an ongoing basis with your tax specialist and/or your accountant.

Conditional Offers

To manage the potential planning risk on developments a lot of your focus may well be on making offers to vendors on a conditional basis. In simple terms this might be offering a price to acquire the property subject to you, the developer, gaining the necessary planning permissions in a certain period of time, at your cost.

Let me illustrate that in a recent case study of EquaGroup.

Case Study – Weybrook House

Weybrook House is a B1A commercial property in the leafy market town of Godalming, just outside Guildford in Surrey.

Having identified the building as having great potential, we approached the vendor with an offer to acquire the property.

Our intention was to convert the property of circa 10,000 sq. ft. into 22 apartments in this tranquil riverside setting.

If we had acquired the property, then applied for the necessary planning permissions and failed at planning, we would have been left with a vacant commercial property and little or no upside development potential.

This is what happened.

We made an offer to acquire the building on a conditional basis, subject to gaining Permitted Development rights determination for 22 apartments.

Following a short period of negotiation, we agreed Heads of Terms to acquire the property for £2.2m on a conditional exchange of contracts.

The conveyancing and funding process took about nine weeks to get to exchange of contracts.

In parallel, we commenced the permitted development process which included full measure of the building, architectural drawings, full flood risk assessment survey and external ground level survey and then submitted our Permitted Development application via our planning consultant.

We did spend a little more time and seed capital on this application due to the location of the property, next to a navigational canal. While the risk was low due to this being a specific navigation canal, we wanted to make sure that the application received a positive and swift outcome.

Sometimes a few weeks extra at the front end saves many months in the long term. After all, this is what we are looking for – anticipating what it takes to create assured outcomes.

As a welcome bonus, permitted development determination was

given ahead of schedule and during the same week we exchanged contracts. This enabled us to maximise the time between exchange

"Sometimes a few weeks extra at the front end saves many weeks or months in the long term"

and legal completion to finalise the funding, commence the detailed design process and commence the tendering for the demolition/ strip out contractor.

The outcome:

- We successfully acquired a great property in Surrey
- We took barely any planning risk at all
- We conditionally exchanged with a £15,000 deposit on a £2.2m property (0.68% !!!)
- We used approximately £5,000 of seed capital for successfully securing permitted development rights determination.
- Successful legal completion followed and the building then went into its development phase, creating 22 beautifully appointed riverside apartments.

The layout below is the existing ground floor layout from the point of purchase of the building which is circa 5,000 sq. ft. gross internal area.

EXISTING GROUND FLOOR PLAN
(scale 1:100)

The following layout is the planned designer's layout of the same floor plate, at the time of this book going to print.

Planning Preparation Costs

Planning costs consist of many parts, vary widely and are specific to the type of planning and scheme you are looking at.

They can be identified as:

- Preparation costs: professional fees and surveys etc.
- Submission costs: statutory planning fees
- Time to get planning: factor the cost of time if you have bought on a bridge for instance!
- Costs of complying with planning: Successful planning decisions may well come with the small print of discharge conditions that must be satisfied. These can vary from approval of cladding and roof tiles to bat surveys and archaeological digs, so watch out for these.
- Levies: Section 106, Community Infrastructure Levy, Affordable Homes
- Costs of appeal: if your planning application is rejected then you may wish to consider the options of appeal with your planning consultant.
- Abortive cost of failure: sunk costs if all planning avenues are rejected.

We will discuss levies, such as Affordable Homes, Section 106

Agreements and Community Infrastructure levies, later.

Most commercial conversion developers will relate mostly to the following two scenarios and their characteristics with regards time, cost and outcome:

Permitted Development Rights scheme

- Preparation time: one-four weeks
- Preparation costs: £1-3k
- Fees £96+VAT
- Determination guidelines: 56 days
- Outcome: Predetermined evaluation criteria with a high probability of a successful outcome, if all guidelines have been followed

Full planning scheme

- Preparation time: 4-12 weeks+
- Preparations costs: £2-20k+
- Fees circa £3-400 per unit (20 units = £6-8k)
- Approval 8-13 weeks as a minimum. However, be prepared for a lengthy period of open-ended discussion (which your planning consultant will help to judge how and when to focus in on a successful outcome or risk a rejection)
- Outcome: variable and highly case specific

Full Planning Permission

Pre-app

If you want to understand the likelihood of securing full planning permission, then a pre-application is an option for you to consider.

The pre-application has a relatively small cost of usually £300 – £1,000 for small to medium schemes and enables you to meet with the planners, face to face, to present and discuss your intentions and gain their feedback for consideration and possible incorporation into your full application at a later date.

Generally, there might be a 2 - 4 week lead time to secure your meeting and then a similar period of time to gain written feedback from the planners.

Importantly, though, the pre-application gives you a litmus test as to what may or may not be acceptable to the planners and how your plans may be received.

It is NOT a legally binding decision and has little reliance value for your full planning submission.

Importantly, it will also have no reliance value to your funders who also understand its lack of weight and will therefore attach no security or valuation uplift to it, until it is replaced with full planning approval.

What it will give you is a clear indication on the considerations that the planning authority are likely to base their decision making process and allow you to get a 'feel' on the likely successful outcome.

Case Study – Kelvedon House

We had experience of a development where we took a measured amount of planning risk on a D1 care home to convert into four apartments and four new-build houses in the rear garden or 'back-lands' as it is often referred to.

We successfully secured planning, however there was some choppy water to navigate through to securing full approval namely:

- Pre-application through a 28-day process which ended up taking 3 ½ months through lack of local authority resource.
- Full planning submission expected to take 13 weeks as a 'major' scheme took a total of 14 months.
- Approval not given under delegated powers but referred to Planning Committee.
- Notice of planning committee date given five days prior to the event.

- Unanimous approval given!

While this was a successful outcome, you can imagine the impact if one had to purchase the property on a short-term bridge or with short-term private investor funds! Therefore be 'eyes wide open' to your overall risk and reward position of full planning and its unpredictable nature.

In fact, some would say that the only predictable thing is the unpredictability!

Minimum Space Standards

The Department of Communities and Local Government formalised, in March 2015, an important document: "Technical Housing Standards – nationally described space standard".

The Standard deals with internal space within new dwellings and sets out requirements for the gross internal floor area (GIA) of new dwellings at a defined level of occupancy, as well as floor areas and dimensions for key parts of the home, notably bedrooms, storage and floor to ceiling height.

The Standard requires that:

1. The dwelling provides at least the gross internal floor area and built-in storage area set out in Table 1 below

2. A dwelling with two or more bedspaces has at least one double (or twin) bedroom

3. In order to provide one bedspace, a single bedroom has a floor area of at least 7.5m2 and is at least 2.15m wide

4. In order to provide two bedspaces, a double (or twin bedroom) has a floor area of at least 11.5m2

5. One double (or twin bedroom) is at least 2.75m wide and every other double (or twin) bedroom is at least 2.55m wide

6. Any area with a headroom of less than 1.5m is not counted within the Gross Internal Area, unless used solely for storage (if the area under the stairs is to be used for storage, assume a general floor area of 1m2 within the Gross Internal Area)

7. Any other area that is used solely for storage and has a head room of 900- 1500mm (such as under eaves) is counted at 50% of its floor area and any area lower than 900mm is not counted at all

8. A built-in wardrobe counts towards the Gross Internal Area and bedroom floor area requirements, but should not reduce the effective width of the room below the minimum widths set out above. The built-in area in excess of 0.72m2 in a double bedroom and 0.36m2 in a single bedroom counts towards the built-in storage requirement

9. The minimum floor to ceiling height is 2.3m for at least 75% of the Gross Internal Area

Number of bedrooms(b)	Number of bed spaces (persons)	1 storey dwellings	2 storey dwellings	3 storey dwellings	Built-in storage
1b	1p	39 (37) *			1.0
	2p	50	58		1.5
2b	3p	61	70		
	4p	70	79		2.0
3b	4p	74	84	90	
	5p	86	93	99	2.5
	6p	95	102	108	
4b	5p	90	97	103	
	6p	99	106	112	
	7p	108	115	121	3.0
	8p	117	124	130	
5b	6p	103	110	116	
	7p	112	119	125	3.5
	8p	121	128	134	
6b	7p	116	123	129	
	8p	125	132	138	4.0

https://assets.publishing.service.gov.uk/government/uploads/system/uploads/attachment_data/file/524531/160519_Nationally_Described_Space_Standard____Final_Web_version.pdf

New full planning applications must comply with these standards.

The advantages to the commercial developer using Permitted Development Rights is that the Minimum Space Standards DO NOT APPLY.

Permitted Development

Permitted Development Rights were first introduced in 2013 and later extended and formalised under The Town and Country Planning (General Permitted Development) (England) (Amendment) Order 2016.

This Order only applies to England and at the time of writing, has not been extended to Wales, Scotland and Northern Ireland.

Permitted Development Rights gives the developer the opportunity, under certain conditions with certain property, the ability to convert commercial property into C3 residential homes within a very short time frame.

Permitted development can take 56 days through guideline periods, however, we have secured this within 44 days! The fee is currently

£96 + VAT and this is irrespective of size of the development.

Current use classes applicable for Permitted Development include:

- B1a offices
- A1 & A2 Retail
- B1c agricultural and light industrial buildings

Discussions abound on how Permitted Development Rights may be extended in the future and areas for inclusion may include:

- Air space
- Sui generis
- Other use classes

All the more reason to engage a great planning consultant to provide a watching brief on developments in this space.

One significant advantage is that under permitted development, minimum space standards do not apply. Hence we can make much more advantageous use of the space within our buildings.

> "under permitted development, minimum space standards do not apply"

Be aware though that mortgage-ability level of apartments begins to become more restricted from lenders when the size of an apartment goes below 30m2, particularly when not in an urban environment, although over time we expect this to relax further as more units come onto the market.

There are restrictions on where Permitted Development can apply and a list of some of these are:

- Conservation Area
- Sites of Special Scientific Interest (SSSI)
- National Park
- Area of Outstanding Natural Beauty (AONB)
- World Heritage Site
- Norfolk or Suffolk Broads
- Listed Buildings – Grade 1 or 2

- Article 4 LPA opt out

Article 4 is more frequently understood by those investing in HMOs. Article 4 is the vehicle that the Local Planning Authority would use to opt out of permitted development and a number of them have done so to date.

The Local Planning Authority will need to be satisfied that your application passes four tests in order to determine your application. These are:

- Transport and highways impacts
- Contamination risks
- Flooding risks
- Impacts of noise from commercial premises on the intended occupiers of the development

Should your application fail (which is unlikely if you have engaged a planning consultant and addressed the predetermined criteria in a diligent manner), then you would review the reasoning and re-apply with the necessary mitigation measures in place to address the concerns.

There are a number of popular areas where Permitted Development Rights apply and some of them are included below in high level summary.

Class M

Development consisting of:

1. A change of use of a building from:

a. a use falling within Class A1 (shops) or Class A2 (financial and professional services) of the Schedule to the Use Classes Order

b. a use as a betting office or pay day loan shop, or

c. a mixed use combining use as a dwellinghouse with:

i: a use as a betting office or pay day loan shop, or

ii: a use falling within either Class A1 (shops) or Class A2 (financial and professional services) of that Schedule

(whether that use was granted permission under Class G of this Part or otherwise)

2. A use falling within Class C3 (dwellinghouses) of that Schedule

3. A building operations reasonably necessary to convert the building, referred to above, to a use falling within Class C3 (dwelling houses) of that Schedule.

Class O

Development consisting of a change of use of a building and any land within its curtilage from a use falling within Class B1(a) (offices) of the Schedule to the Use Classes Order, to a use falling within Class C3 (dwelling houses) of that Schedule.

Development is not permitted by Class O if:

1. The building is on article 2(5) land;

2. The building was not used for a use falling within Class B1(a) (offices) of the Schedule to the Use Classes Order—

   a. On 29th May 2013, or

   b. In the case of a building which was in use before that date but was not in use on that date, when it was last in use;

3. The use of the building falling within Class C3 (dwelling houses) of that Schedule was begun after 30th May 2016;

4. The site is, or forms part of, a safety hazard area

5. The site is, or forms part of, a military explosives storage area

6. The building is a listed building or is within the curtilage of a listed building or

7. The site is, or contains, a scheduled monument

Conditions

Development under Class O is permitted subject to the condition that before beginning of the development, the developer must apply to the local planning authority for a determination as to whether the prior approval of the authority will be required as to:

1. Transport and highways impacts of the development
2. Contamination risks on the site
3. Flooding risks on the site and the provisions of paragraph W (prior approval) apply in relation to that application

Development under Class O is permitted, subject to the condition that it must be completed within a period of three years starting with the prior approval date.

Class P

Temporary permitted development rights also apply in respect of the change of use of premises from B8 'storage and distribution' use under 500m2 to C3 'residential use'.

This is subject to a number of criteria being met and subject to Prior Approval being sought in respect of air quality, transport and highways impacts, contamination risks, flooding risks, noise impact, and impact on the sustainability of adjoining uses.

For a property to benefit from C3 use, the prior approval date must be before 10 June 2019 and the development must be completed within three years of the prior approval date. (The 'prior approval date' is the date that the developer successfully completes the prior approval process).

Class PA

Development consisting of a change of use of a building and any land within its curtilage from a use falling within Class B1(c) (light industrial) of the Schedule to the Use Classes Order to a use falling within Class C3 (dwelling houses) of that Schedule.

Class PA is not permitted if

- Application was before 30th September 2017
- Building was not used solely for a light industrial use on 19th March 2014
- Prior approval date falls on or after 1st October 2020

- Gross floor space of the existing building exceeds 500 square meters
- Site under agricultural tenancy
- Agricultural tenancy over the site has been terminated UNLESS landlord and tenant agree site is not required for agricultural purposes

Restrictions would also apply if the site is:

- Site of special scientific interest
- A safety hazard area
- Military explosives storage area
- The building is a listed building or is within the curtilage of a listed building; or the site is, or contains, a scheduled monument

Class PA IS permitted subject to before beginning the development:

- Building was solely light industrial on 19 March 2014
- Apply for a determination on prior approval
  - transport and highways impacts
  - contamination risks
  - flooding risks
- LPA considers an adverse impact on sustainability of important:
  - industrial services or storage
  - distribution services
- Must be completed within a period of 3 years from approval

As mentioned earlier, the Minimum Housing Standards do not apply to permitted development applications and therefore the developer can be much more creative in increasing the density of apartments and therefore maximizing space to serve a different market.

Class Q

Agricultural buildings are permitted to change to C3 use (dwelling houses) together with some building operations reasonably necessary to facilitate the conversion, subject to meeting certain criteria:

- No more than five separate dwelling houses can be developed under this Class.

- Subject to this limit of five dwelling houses, up to three can be 'larger dwelling houses'. (A larger single dwelling house is one with a floor space of more 100m2). No more than 465m2 of floor space can change use to 'larger dwelling houses' under this class and no more than 465m2 of residential floor space is allowed in larger dwelling houses.

- Within the overall limit of five dwelling houses, up to five can be 'smaller dwelling houses'. (Smaller dwelling houses each have a floor space of no more than 100m2).

It is also subject to Prior Approval being sought in respect of transport and highways impacts, noise impact, contamination risks, flooding risks, location or siting and the design or external appearance of the building.

Agricultural buildings under 500m2 are permitted to change to a flexible commercial use, comprising A1, A2, A3, B1, B8, C1 or D2 uses. This is subject to meeting certain criteria and Prior Approval being sought in relation to uses over 150m2 in respect of transport and highways impacts, noise impact, contamination risks and flooding risks.

Agricultural buildings within land under 500m2 are permitted to change to a state funded school or a registered nursery. This is subject to meeting certain criteria and Prior Approval being sought in respect of transport and highways impacts, noise impact, contamination risks, flooding risks and whether the building is suitable for the proposed use.

If your proposal meets the permitted development requirements but you are unsure, for peace of mind you may choose to apply for a lawful development certificate (LDC). This is not the same as planning permission but is proof that your building work is lawful.

Permitted Development Summary

So to summarise, the advantages of permitted development for the developer's consideration:

- There is a clear process of determination
- The costs to get approval are very low
- The outcome has a very high level of probability
- The timescales are widely known and predictable
- Levies such as S106, CIL and Affordable Homes almost certainly will not apply
- No minimum space requirements for apartments
- Minimum determining factors
    - Transport and highways impacts
    - Contamination risks
    - Flooding risks
    - Impacts of noise from commercial premises on the
    - intended occupiers of the development
- Parking is not a requirement (subject to satisfying the criteria above)
- Short timescales enable increased effectiveness of engagement with vendor conditionality
- Private investor engagement streamlined as much reduced levels of risk compared to full planning
- Overall speed of the process to accessing your returns!

In a recent development scheme for 16 apartments with a GDV of circa £2.65m, we secured the B1A commercial property on a conditional basis (subject to gaining permitted development).

The preparation for the submission took 10 days and the costs of professional fees was £650 + VAT.

"ensure you have clarity on exactly what use class the commerical property you are targeting, is"

The application was £80 (this has now risen to £96 so beware of the £16 hidden price increases!) + VAT.

The 56-day guidelines for determination for a permitted development application provided a nice surprise when Colchester approved the scheme within 44 days.

Subsequently we have had a similar application based on a 26-apartment conversion of a B1A office building confirmed in 56 days, in the same city.

As permitted development is getting used more frequently we are seeing a number of local authorities starting to express resource shortages and timescales starting to drift in certain cases. However, we have not experienced a reduced level of success which is the main criteria, during what is still a relatively short process, given the contingency periods we will always add to our programme timelines.

Building use

An important factor is to ensure you have clarity on exactly what use class the commercial property you are targeting, is.

This may seem obvious but, yet again, it is where your planning consultant will come into their own in researching the correct lawful usage class of the property.

They will research the history for:

- Previous planning applications
- Change of use
- Current and previous occupational use
- Commercial leases
- Business rates from the Valuation Office Agency (VOA)
- Enquiries to current/previous owners
- Any additional documentation in the public domain

This research and outcome can be the difference between identifying a building with potential for permitted development rights and full planning.

Planning Obligations & Levies

Discussions about planning obligations should take place as early as possible in the planning process, including at the pre-application stage. This will prevent delays in finalising those planning applications which are granted, subject to the completion of planning obligation agreements.

Planning Obligations are used for three purposes, to:

- Prescribe
- Compensate
- Mitigate

Most commonly they are used to secure affordable housing, and to specify the type and timing of this housing and to secure financial contributions to provide infrastructure or affordable housing.

A planning obligation can be subject to conditions; it can specify restrictions definitely or indefinitely and in terms of payments, the timing of these can be specified in the obligation.

Section 106

Section 106 of the Town and Country Planning Act 1990 are agreements which are linked to the planning process and are planning obligations of the eventual planning permission once granted. They are a legal agreement between the applicant of the planning permission and the local planning authority. The purpose of the section 106 is to mitigate the impact of your new home on the local community and infrastructure and enable contributions towards the costs of providing community and social infrastructure, the need for which has arisen as a result of a new development taking place.

The land itself, rather than the person or organisation that develops the land, is bound by a Section 106 Agreement, something any future owners will need to take into account.

If the Section 106 is not complied with, it is enforceable against the person that entered into the obligation and any subsequent owner.

The Section 106 can be enforced by injunction.

Section 106 obligations can:

a. Secure affordable housing in the local area

b. Restrict the development or use of the land in any specified way

c. Require specified operations or activities to be carried out in, on, under or over the land

d. Require the land to be used in any specified way

e. Require a sum or sums to be paid to the authority (or, to the Greater London Authority) on a specified date or dates or periodically

In case of a breach of the obligation, the authority can take direct action and recover expenses.

The planning obligation is a formal document, a deed, which states that it is an obligation for planning purposes, identifies the relevant land, the person entering the obligation, their interest and the relevant local authority that would enforce the obligation. The obligation can be a unitary obligation or multi-party agreement.

The obligation becomes a land charge and the tests are:

a. Necessary to make the development acceptable in planning terms

b. Directly related to the development

c. Fairly and reasonably related in scale to the development

Community Infrastructure Levy

The Community Infrastructure Levy (CIL) is a Planning charge under Planning Act 2008 and became Effective 6 April 2010 - Community Infrastructure Levy Regulations 2010.

Developments may be liable if your local planning authority has chosen to set a charge in its area. The money is used to support development by funding infrastructure that the council, local community and neighbourhoods need, such as schools or transport improvements - which are needed to support new homes and businesses in the areas.

The CIL receipts must be used to fund, provide, improve, operate or maintain infrastructure.

CIL is non-negotiable, but there are certain exceptions where relief may be available, such as affordable housing and developments by charities and those used for charitable purposes.

The amount to be paid is based on the net floor area of a new building or extension and its use. It will apply to most new buildings and extensions over 100sq m gross and to new homes regardless of their floor area.

The following link provides more detail into the process and inner workings of CIL.

https://www.gov.uk/guidance/community-infrastructure-levy#charging-schedule-overarch-section

Affordable Housing Contribution

Every local authority is responsible for drawing up their own policy within the regulatory framework guidelines deciding on the objectives, factors and contributions required.

The contribution can come in a number of forms, however is usually either:

• Allocation of housing units or
• Cash payment to the local authority

As an example, below is an excerpt from Mole Valley District, Council's Strategy and Policy document, which gives a clear illustration of their identification, needs and deployment in their area of responsibility.

1. *In order to increase the provision of affordable homes the Council will aim to secure a minimum of 950 net affordable units within the District between the period 2006 and 2026 (contributing towards the sub-regional target of 40% of all new homes being affordable).*

2. *In order to achieve this target the District Council will require where viable:*

- *that on all housing development of 1 to 9 gross dwellings, financial contribution equivalent to providing 20% of the total number of dwellings as affordable is made.*

- *that on all housing developments of 10 to 14 gross dwellings, 30% of the total number of dwellings are affordable.*

- *that on all housing developments of 15 gross dwellings or more, 40% of the total number of dwellings are affordable.*

3. *On sites of 10 or more gross dwellings, on-site provision should be made and must incorporate a mix of dwelling types and sizes which reflect the site's characteristics, the development as a whole and the type of need identified in the most up-to-date Housing Needs Survey and Strategic Housing Market Assessment.*

4. *Affordable housing provision must also incorporate a mix of tenures. The Council will negotiate the exact tenure split on each site. However, the presumption is that at least 50% of the total number of affordable homes provided on site will be for social rented accommodation. Where the Council considers it is appropriate, a higher level of social rented accommodation may be sought.*

5. *Small scale affordable housing schemes may be acceptable on an exceptional basis on sites outside of, but adjoining the settlement boundaries of, the rural villages.*

When Affordable Housing is Required		
Units	Urban	Rural
1-5	None, unless development is greater than 1000sqm combined gross floorspace in which case a financial contribution will be required	None, unless development is greater than 1000sqm combined gross floorspace in which case a financial contribution will be required
6-9	None, unless development is greater than 1000sqm combined gross floorspace in which case a financial contribution will be required	Financial contribution
10	None, unless development is greater than 1000sqm combined gross floorspace in which case a financial contribution will be required	30% of units on-site
11-14	30% of units on-site	30% of units on-site
15+	40% of units on-site	40% of units on-site

http://www.molevalley.gov.uk/media/pdf/n/h/Affordable_Housing_SPD_Jan_2018_update_FINAL.pdf

Vacant Building Credit

Vacant Building Credits provide an incentive for brownfield development on sites containing vacant buildings. Where a vacant building is brought back into any lawful use, or is demolished to be replaced by a new building, the developer can benefit from a financial credit, equivalent to the existing gross floor space of relevant vacant buildings when the local planning authority calculates any affordable housing contribution which will be sought.

Affordable housing contributions may be required for any increase in floor space and the Vacant Building Credit applies to on-site affordable housing, as well as financial contributions to off-site provision. However, the Vacant Building Credit does not apply where the building has been abandoned.

The application will require the Gross External Area (GEA) to be formally measured and signed off by a RICS Chartered Surveyor or RIBA member

"**Vacant Building Credits provide an incentive for brownfield development on sites containing vacant buildings**"

architect.

The policy is intended to incentivise brownfield development, including the reuse or redevelopment of empty and redundant buildings. In considering how the vacant building credit should apply to a particular development, local planning authorities should have regard to the intention of national policy.

In doing so, it may be appropriate for authorities to consider:

- Whether the building has been made vacant for the sole purposes of redevelopment

- Whether the building is covered by an existing or recently expired planning permission for the same, or substantially the same development.

An example might be:

Vacant building Gross External Area: 4,500 m2

Proposed Building Gross External Areas: 6,750 m2

The Affordable Housing contribution would be 33.3% of what would normally be expected.

https://www.gov.uk/guidance/planning-obligations

Pause for thought - How sensitive are you?

We are all sensitive - some to a greater level than others but what about your Development?

Do you know exactly how sensitive your development is and more importantly - to what?

A few simple steps below will guide you to a clearer understanding of all the moving parts of your Business - because that is what a development is, with lots of interconnecting parts.

So here is your 5-Step Sensitivity Analysis Start-up:

1. Understand ALL the variables that your development could face
2. Model how sensitive your goals (profit/cash/outcome etc) are and how they would be affected by changes in each variable in turn, as well as multiple variables at the same time
3. Identify the ones you can address
4. Plan a mitigation strategy to reduce, eliminate or transfer risk
5. Monitor residual risk remaining and repeat the review regularly

I have used this on £1 - 100m+ developments over nearly three decades with complex simulations. While these were necessarily sophisticated, the reality is the basics are not hard to follow IF you understand the process and logic behind them.

Understanding variables, sensitivity and risk management is a foundation system in your property business and can save - and make you - £10,000's.

Follow this simple 5 step plan above to help you better understand your developments and businesses and safeguard from many risks materialising announced.

6. Valuation

Don't wish it were easier, wish you were better –
Jim Rohn

"ensure the truth doesn't emerge AFTER the costs have been spent!"

A deep understanding of the valuation process is extremely important to ensure that your hard-earned working capital has not been deployed on the valuation itself, as well as other expense items, with a strong possibility of a poor valuation materialising. We are looking for assured outcomes after all!

As I often say, ensure the truth doesn't emerge AFTER the costs have been spent!

The valuation process and indeed the valuation report is important to a number of parties:

1. You - it is important to you to understand that your due diligence stands on good ground.

2. Your funder - It's extremely important to your commercial funder that they hold an independent report assessing all crucial elements of your development which will enable them to assess its suitability as security.

3. Your private investor - Your investor(s) may wish to review the valuation as part of their due diligence process.

When should you undertake a valuation report? This is a bit of a holy grail question. You may wish to deploy a valuation report very early on in the process to ensure your seed capital being deployed is not wasted and you have a valuation report that supports your assessment. Therefore, you can be confident to expend other costs, such as legal and the survey costs with a heightened sense of confidence in the numbers. The downside of doing a valuation report at this stage is that this may not be a valuation that the funder will rely on and therefore the process may need to be repeated. The earlier you can identify your funder, the earlier you can access their panel of valuation surveyors.

RICS Red Book

So what is a valuation report? The valuation report is governed by strict standards from the Royal Institute of Chartered Surveyor (RICS). They have particular standards referred to as a Red Book valuation and the purpose of these standards are to ensure that valuations produced by RICS members achieve high standards of integrity, clarity and objectivity and are reported in accordance with recognised basis appropriate for the purpose.

The standards define:

1. Criteria used to establish whether members are appropriately qualified.
2. Steps necessary to deal with any actual perceived threat to their independence and objectivity.
3. Matters to be addressed when agreeing conditions of engagement.
4. Basis of valuation, assumptions and material considerations must be taken into account when preparing a valuation.
5. Minimum reporting standards.
6. Matters that shall be disclosed when valuations may be relied upon by third parties.

The RICS Red Book Valuation is a highly governed document undertaken by professionals.

Who relies on the Red Book Valuation? You will rely to a certain extent on the Red Book Valuation and your private investors may have a significant interest. It is primarily your commercial funder who will be interested in the Red Book Valuation. This will be a critical gateway and component of their bank grade due diligence, which they will be required to take to their internal credit committee, to get sign off for your final credit approved offer.

The common challenges that are experienced by many developers are surprises with down valuations. What exactly is a down valuation? Well simply put, it is when the valuer says that the development economics are less than you had envisaged. This may be due to:

- Reduced GDV
- Increased construction costs expected
- Additional professional fees anticipated
- Additional time required
- Additional contingency required
- Property value less than expected

Whilst these are difficult situations, certain measures can be taken to improve your due diligence early in the process and to walk a mile in the valuer's shoes to enable a closer correlation later, during your development's timeline, so that you are more aligned with what the funder is likely to lend, based on the valuation results.

Any significant down valuation will be potentially highly disruptive to your development. At a worst case, the valuation may spell doom to the project and you will lose any costs or seed capital if you cannot find somebody else who may be interested in that development.

Therefore, it makes business sense to invest a significant amount of time to equip yourself with the knowledge and skills to incorporate the systematic process and techniques of a Red Book Valuation, in your development's due diligence. The power of anticipation at work!

If there is a down valuation and therefore less funds will be loaned by the commercial funder, then it will be your capital or your private investor's capital which makes up the rest. Hence a down valuation will mean an increased requirement in private capital and therefore, assuming profitability remains the same, this will correlate to a reduction in return on capital employed on the private investor's returns.

"equip yourself with the knowledge and skills to incorporate the systematic process and techniques of a Red Book Valuation, in your development's due diligence"

What would a RICS Red Book Valuation have within its contents?

1. Executive summary. This will give an outline of the findings at a high level and enable you to quickly capture the essence of the document.

2. Instructions and terms of reference. This will outline the specific instructions that an RICS surveyor is working under, the background of the appointment and the purpose.

3. Property statutory and legal aspects. This will cover all areas such as location, situation, any description on the property, the condition of the property, town planning and its current situation, taxation, environmental impact and consideration, any statutory matters, tenure and condition of commercial leases and the occupational lease arrangements.

4. Development proposals. This would give a detailed description of the intentions of the developer and their proposed development plans with regards to this site. The proposed construction and accommodation that is being provided, whether that be new homes, new-build apartments or refurbished apartments etc. The construction proposal will include the type of construction, the method, the duration, how the construction is going to be procured, the proposed specification of the final units, its intended purpose and any levies, which would be Section 106, CIL agreements, Affordable Homes.

5. Market commentary. This would include a market overview of the national markets, of the local market, any information from the RICS housing market surveys and any recent comparable sales transactions of similar properties in a similar area, probably within a 0.5 – 1 km radius.

6. The valuation. This will be at a number of levels. This will look at the valuation considerations that are being taken into account, the approach to how the valuation is being undertaken, any residual appraisals, the valuation itself and also for insurance purposes, the reinstatement costs of the property.

7. Security for the loan. This will give an overview as to how appropriate the property will be as security for the loan being

provided by your commercial lender.

8. Any general assumptions and conditions for the valuations.

9. Detailed set of appendices which will include the letter of instruction, any detail of layouts, floor plans, elevations, any background residential information that was being relied upon, the developer valuation, development valuation and then a detailed assessment of the basis of the valuation and its assumptions.

As you can see, this is a detailed report and may be anywhere from 50 to 100 pages long, even longer on larger developments.

Anybody can instruct an RICS valuation report as long as they can provide the access to the property. Predominantly the three parties that would instruct would be yourself as a developer, your funder and possibly your private investor. However, your private investor may be happy to rely on your developer's valuation or a transparent sight of the funders Red Book valuation.

As a developer, whether you have instructed an RICS valuation or not, the lender will always want to instruct one themselves. The RICS valuation must be produced under the instruction of the funder and addressed to the funder. In certain cases, the funder may allow an existing RICS valuation report to be re-directed in the name of the funder. However, this is rare and most credit committees would insist on a brand new instruction.

As a developer, that leaves a decision to be made very early on, on whether to invest in a valuation, knowing full well that a further valuation will be required by your chosen funder and possibly a further valuation from your mezzanine funder, if you choose that route also. One would hope your commercial broker can make arrangements whereby your mezzanine funder would be content to stand by your senior debt funder's RICS valuation. However, again a revised fee may be required for a rewrite/re-instruction of that valuation in the name of the mezzanine funder.

The strong inference here is to move swiftly in deciding the senior debt funder you wish to proceed with as early as your due diligence allows.

The valuation report is undertaken by an RICS surveyor which can be a local regional practice or can be one of the larger national practices. Each party will have a different level of professional indemnity cover, which is an important criteria of the evaluation of the lender in selecting their surveyors. The commercial funders will typically have a panel of RICS surveyors to choose from - typically, between three and five. You will have the choice in discussions with your funder and broker, to select which surveyor from the commercial funder's surveying panel you wish to instruct.

The instruction will always come from the lender and in doing so the report will be addressed back to the lender. You should expect that the developer will be responsible for paying for the valuation report and this would usually happen at the time of instruction, rather than at the time that the lending facility is approved and drawn down. This will have an impact on your cash flow and should be factored in at day one of your due diligence. Typical RICS Red Book valuation reports can vary from £1,500 up to £10,000, and can go much higher on larger developments. All figures excluding VAT. The range will be dependent on where in the country this is instructed, the type of practice, the amount of professional indemnity insurance requested, the scale, size and complexity of the scheme involved.

In the appraisal summary, often in the appendices, the scheme will have the computations recorded. These elements which will be assessed include:

- Sales valuation units
- Cost per square foot
- Unit price gross sales
- Ground rents
- Ancillary - parking and storage areas as examples.
- Net expected realisation

There will then be a detailed assessment of the outlay costs, which will include:

- Acquisition costs
- Stamp duty

- Agent fees
- Legal fees
- Construction costs
- Contingency assessment, frequently between 7.5-15%.
- Other construction costs, which may well include items such as utilities.

There will be professional fees. These can include:

- Structural engineer
- Quantity surveyor
- Architect
- Project manager
- Mechanical and electrical engineer
- Acoustics
- CDM and health and safety
- Marketing and letting costs for the marketing of the units to be sold
- Disposal fees
- Sales agent's fees
- Legal fees
- New home warranties
- Show home costs
- EPC costs.

"Simulate the Red Book Valuation in your development"

There will be then an assessment of funding costs and funding rates, for the land, the construction and that will give a total cost. This will give you a very clear understanding of how the RICS valuer has assessed the development and the funder will take this into account as they make a final offer in principle term sheet, to go to credit.

If these look familiar then they should! Simulate the Red Book valuation in your development analyser.

Take time to look through all of these elements and then review your development analyser and decide if it is comprehensive enough to simulate the Red Book Valuation process.

Timing

The dilemma for any investor is when to make the instruction for a valuation report, either direct or via your lender. Timing is crucial. It must happen before exchange of contracts, unless you're buying in cash and choose not to have a survey done, which would not be recommended. At the point of exchange, you would want to have absolute clarity on your funder's position. Do not exchange contracts unless you are clear you have all the key components in place to fund the transaction through to completion.

The dilemma for developers is by investing in the valuation too early, you potentially have duplicate costs because your funder will want a valuation report redone later down the process. If you do it too late, you may have abortive costs if the development becomes unfundable.

"understanding the due diligence"

One point to make with the RICS Red Book Valuation process is they work off current and historical information only and not future forecast information. While they might note certain trends and observations on how the market may be moving, their reliance data will always be based on historic demonstrable costs that have been realised in the market and not on a future assessment of where the market may or may not be going.

When you are understanding the due diligence of one of your developments, look at how a lender will instruct the valuation and how the valuer will look at that. The valuer has a professional job to do and will be putting his professional indemnity insurance on the line with his report. They will look at it realistically and it will not be a racy valuation. It's important for you to understand that in your due diligence.

You may choose to look at having a range of values on your GDV. We have a:

- Low end – supported by Red Book Valuation
- Medium – midway between low and high
- High end – based on where local agents predict the market might be at point of marketing

The best advice is always to under promise and over deliver!

Note that when you are designing your building there are certain elements in the valuation process that can impact the valuation level of each one of your units. These might include the floor level that the unit is on, the orientation and the aspect of each apartment as an example. Be aware of this at the design stage and you may be able to optimise your scheme.

Monitoring Surveyor Report

Most development finance lenders will wish to add a further layer of due diligence to the process by engaging with an independent Quantity Surveyor (QS) or Monitoring Surveyor as they are known. They will be engaged from a panel of surveyors that the funder holds, in a similar way to that of the Red Book Valuation process. It will also come as no surprise that you as the developer will be responsible for the cost of this report also, which can vary between £1,500 -£4,000+ depending on the size of the development.

The monitoring surveyor report will cover the following areas:

- Planning consents and approvals
- Building control
- Listed building consents and approvals
- Health and safety
- Development plans and specification
- Contracts, appointments and responsibilities
- Assessment of risks

- Construction/refurbishment budget
- Programme assessment
- Contingency review
- Main contractor assessment
- Collateral warranties
- Professional team
- Insurances
- Overall scheme economics
- Development appraisal
- Cash flow analysis

Once the development is funded and underway, the development finance will be drawn down on a monthly basis in arrears, based on value of certified work done.

It will be the monitoring surveyor, who originated the aforementioned due diligence report, who will also attend site every month and check the application for funding draw down against the work done to date and sign off as appropriate. The fees for your budget for this monitoring surveyor function will be between £750-£1,500 per month of the construction programme and probably higher on larger developments.

> "the development finance will be drawn down on a monthly basis in arrears based on value of certified work done"

During the development at each of these monthly meetings the Monitoring Surveyor will also monitor the construction programme and compliance – in short, is everything on time, budget and quality? If any of these factors are not running entirely to expectation it will be monitored closely and reasoning sought as to why and an understanding of what the plan is to resolve.

Intervention measures can be requested should issues exist. For instance, if there are cost over-runs through variations on the main contractor account and these are deemed to have absorbed and removed most of the contingency available, then the Monitoring Surveyor can recommend to the lender that the developer injects further capital into the development to restore the contingency 'buffer' in the development finances.

This process should be monitored religiously each month to ensure that this scenario is managed effectively and never allowed to occur, as injecting additional capital into the development is going to be painful for developer and private investors alike.

In EquaGroup our process for detailed design and specification production at the front end of a development is undertaken with much care and attention. It is driven into the procurement phase so that we are mitigating as far as possible the opportunity for main contractors to request variations and extensions of time.

Allow sufficient time in your programme to get your design and contracts detailed and effective at the start, enabling contract award time and cost to closely mirror final account end turn out positions with minimum variations.

Remember, a design change on paper at design and tendering phase costs nothing, but during the construction phase it can be extremely expensive!

Mixed Use Valuation

As developers we may be interested in property with existing or future mixed use development potential. This may be existing shops with uppers which may be converted to residential and many other permutations. After all, permitted development enables us to gain determination to convert retail units under 150 sq. m from a shop (A1) or financial and professional services (A2) use class to C3 residential, relatively simply.

It may be our intention to hold the commercial element that remains post conversion in a property/investment company, or it could be sold to the open market. Whichever our strategy, it will involve leases and commercial finance, hence a different valuation process is required.

It is common sense, as well as an established standard of valuation, that the front of a shop – the part seen by passers-by – is worth more than the back. It follows that a shop with 15m of frontage and a depth of 8m commands a higher rent than a shop of 8m frontage and depth of 15m.

Zoning

Zoning is a standard method of measuring retail premises to calculate and compare their value and is used by both public and private sector surveyors with the principle being that the front band of space is valued at one rate, the next band at half that, and so on.

Its is commonly referred to as ITZA - In terms of Zone A

Whilst zoning valuations do vary, the most common is to take the first three bands – called Zone A, Zone B and Zone C – at 6m depths into the shop, calling all remaining areas of the shop Zone D, and value ancillary space on an ad-hoc basis.

Shop or retail premises are divided into a number of zones each of a depth of 6.1 metres which equates to 20 feet which is where the origination of this methodology comes from back in the 1950's.

Zone A closest to the front window is most valuable with the value decreasing with distance from the frontage: Zone B is the next 6.1 metres, then Zone C until the entire depth of the retail area is allocated to a zone - anything after Zone C is usually defined as the remainder.

ZONE	VALUE ITZA
A	A
B	A/2
C	A/4
D	A/8
Basement	A/10

Mixed Use Zoning example

This example describes the valuation of a retail unit with an 8m frontage to the street and has a depth of 22.3m. Given that each zone consists of 6.1m there would therefore be 4 zones to value in this retail unit.

ZONE	MEASURES	ACTUAL (M2)	ITZA (N2)
A	8m x 6.1m	48.8	48.8
B	8m x 6.1m	48.8	24.4
C	8m x 6.1m	48.8	12.2
D	8m x 4m	32	4
		178.4	89.4

Using local comparables if we assume a rate of £1,050/m² ITZA can be established, then a valuation for this retail unit would be £93,870 per annum.

Pause for thought - Your Personal Audit Trail is Permanent

Your future investor, business/joint venture partner or funder may know a lot about you before YOU ever realise.

In today's social media and Google-driven society, every step you take and words you say will leave a hallmark on your brand. Whether at Companies House, photos on social media or words on Facebook posts, your actions speak just as loudly as words. Remember your reader may not get your context either!

Having been involved in global corporate troubleshooting over many years, I know how perception is extremely hard to counteract in the world of brand recognition, personal credibility and due diligence.

The largest investor you never had will in all likelihood be the one you never realised existed. They may have been turned off by something you said, something you did and something that does not authentically align with their values.

Someone said to me once that they had been watching me quietly from afar for almost a year before approaching for mentoring.

Being authentic is incredibly important - it oozes through every pore in everything you do - and is accentuated during the good times and particularly in the tough times.

A bit like alcohol in some regards - having a few beers can make some loud, some fall asleep or some react aggressively etc - is this revealing their true inner personality or creating a new personality as a reaction?

Remember our opinion is less relevant but walking a mile in your future funder's shoes, to think how they may perceive you, is wise. How would your potential partner in the future perceive you to be by each action?

Your private investor will not necessarily expect perfection, but they will expect transparency and great communication, an acute sense of anticipation, forward planning and also a solid resoluteness of someone they would welcome in the trenches with them, side by side, should the 'proverbial' hit the fan!

I spent 26 years in corporate life and have witnessed how corporate culture likes to mould you into what it wants you to be - akin to wrapping you in cling-film. It can and does suck the life out of many people.

Cast aside the cling-film and live life and breathe!! Be who you are, be authentic, be proud and grow wings and flourish.

Think twice about jeopardising your reputation through a careless act, omission, or poor choice of words. Your personal audit trail is indelible and will propel or anchor you - which do you choose?

7. Funding

Nothing great was ever achieved without enthusiasm - Randolph Emerson

For many, the raising of finance for their commercial conversion represents one of the most significant challenges for them to get their heads around. Without a doubt, if you can understand clearly and navigate the processes, systems and due diligence required to successfully fund your commercial conversion, you will unlock a world of potential that can indeed be life-changing. However, in order to do this, you must follow a set of systems, processes and engage with professionals to support you in securing the crucial credit line to unlock your development.

I have mentioned commercial finance a number of times in this book and it is woven into every stage in our processes of due diligence. The world of commercial finance can be complex and there are many options. Therefore, it is important to appoint a commercial broker, as part of our professional team.

When looking for the right commercial broker, you must take into account a number of things:

1. Their experience.
2. Their area of expertise in particular types of commercial finance and development.
3. Their location and previous work in particular geographical areas.
4. Their credibility and references.
5. Access to the continually moving commercial finance market.
6. Personal connection you have with them as there will be some significant trust, challenge and handholding in equal measure here!

The right commercial broker is certainly worth their weight in gold. Commercial finance is a specialist field. My recommendation for getting the best out of your commercial broker is to be extremely open with them. In order for a commercial broker to serve you in the best way possible, they need to understand and

"woven into every stage in our processes of due diligence"

walk a mile in your shoes! They can give advice and counsel on your strategy and they can deploy significant enquiries into the market to help you unlock the potential of your development. They need to be very clear, as do the funders, on your exit strategy for your development, which could be a buy-develop-sell, a buy-develop-hold or a hybrid solution etc.

Commercial brokers will understand the importance of due diligence at all stages of the process. They will understand and support you in the process, being realistic and clear. The broker must understand how you intend to fund the development and that will include where the balance of the funds are going to be sourced from (retained profits, own funds, private investors etc).

The first area of due diligence you will be required to draw together will be that of yourself. Know Your Customer (KYC) is critical information in the due diligence process. You must provide this information, so keep it relevant and updated at all times, pre-prepared and placed in a Dropbox (or similar) and include all information on each director of the company, which may include:

- Assets and the liability schedule
- CV of each director
- Certified proof of ID (passport/driving license/firearms certificate) - keep certification within 3 months old
- Certified proof of address (driving license/utility bill/bank statement) and keep certification within 3 months old
- List of your previous directorships
- Bank account statements
- Company accounts
- Criminal history
- Property portfolio experience
- Anti-Money Laundering (AML) checks
- Credit checks
- Origination of funds
- Business plan – increasingly being requested by banks

Your CV should include a list of all relevant information that supports your application and your experience. It should include due diligence on your company. This could be your SPV company that may have already been set up.

If that is a brand new clean title SPV, then that is fine. However, lenders certainly, for first-time lending, may also require some extra background on your overall strategy - who you are as an overarching business and what your aspirations are. It is useful to provide that information to give them context. In certain cases, this may also include any progress reports, company reports and financial accounts, as well as a list with case studies of any portfolio properties that you currently own.

As you can see, all this information is readily accessible and can be prepared in advance by you. On presentation of this information through Dropbox to your broker, it will ensure that you are seen, in part, with credibility and show them that you have the presence of mind, courtesy and foresight to walk a mile in the funder's and the broker's shoes and this will go down well with the funder and enable them to perform their role more efficiently. If you have any queries, seek their advice and continually involve and improve this Dropbox to make it easier as your development projects evolve continuously.

I suggest that you save through Dropbox or any other file-sharing platform, the due diligence of your particular development. This would include layouts, drawings, plans, agent's literature, your due diligence sheets, comparables, any information from the builders and surveys - all the required information in one place that is readily accessible.

Your funder needs to know this information, as could be the case for your private investors and also your solicitor whose client account will be receiving the transfer of funds.

Increased Know Your Customer and Anti-Money Laundering checks are meaning that this information is required at the earliest stages through your broker and certainly prior to any issue of credit backed terms. It is best to set this expectation early with your potential private investors who will be required to provide:

- Name of individual/company investing
- Proof of address
- Director and shareholder details
- Certified KYC for directors and major shareholders
- Proof of origination of investment funds

Commercial funding can be complex for your commercial conversion. However there are a number of different options that are frequently used, which include the following: bridge finance, commercial and development finance, bank loans and 100% loan-to-cost funding as well as new entrant models from time to time. Let us take each of these in turn.

Bridge finance

Bridge finance can be expensive, however, it also can be quick to ascertain and transact. It is ideal for swift purchases and quite often, the lending criteria can be broader than most of the senior debt facilities. Bridge funding will always take a first charge on the property in question and will loan typically anything up to 65% loan-to-value - note it is very important to look at what loan to value actually means in this case, they will always look at what the asset currently is and what evidence it has, not what it could be in the future. They see loan-to-current value and not GDV.

"your private capital cannot be phased as it will almost certainly be required on day one of property purchase"

Typically, you will be charged a fee going into the deal at a certain percentage, possibly 0.75% to 2%. There will also be management, legal, valuation and administration fees. There may also be an 'exit' fee of circa 0% to 2%. Read the small print as in this case it can be based on loan-to-cost, or it can be based on GDV. There will be a monthly interest charge, which on a per annum basis, may be anywhere from 9% to 24% usually charged on a per calendar month basis.

Commercial and development finance

With a senior debt facility, you can secure funding for the development and for the property itself in isolation. Now, at this stage, it becomes very apparent that there can be a battle of the security charges and we'll come to this later on. However, for the purposes of this book, we will focus on the combination of commercial and development finance from one provider.

Generally, the development finance for the development/ construction process would attract somewhere between 80% and 100% costs funded and the funding of the purchase of the property might typically be between 40% to 70% of the property itself.

The bank view your private capital as your 'pain' money which must be put in first, ahead of their funding.

This will give a very clear indication that your private capital cannot be phased as it will almost certainly be required on day one of property purchase.

Bank loan

The bank loan can be a very flexible form of finance and extremely versatile in business. This type of finance has a different risk consideration and is generally not utilised for property transactions involving development.

It is, however, useful for working capital or a specific business plan. For example, if one were acquiring a bed and breakfast or a hotel property and then wanted to run it as a serviced accommodation block where revenue modelling and business plan assumptions are an underlying part of the business plan.

100% loan-to-cost funding

This is a particularly specialised area. Generally, it will have a very different structure and feel to your normal considerations. This type of funding provider, quite often backed by family funds, may cover up to 100% of the costs associated with the property purchase and the property development. They tend to have a minimum and a maximum threshold on GDV, quite often require planning approval to be in place and therefore, will not take planning risk.

They will start to get interested in projects where you have secured your position, i.e. offer accepted, exclusivity period, possibly even exchange. They may have focus in certain limited areas, and they will certainly have a profit threshold, where there must be a profit to GDV percentage potentially. For example, as a minimum, 75% cost to GDV. The structuring of these type of loan agreements tends to be very different, whereby your development will actually be purchased in the funder's SPV, and you will have a contract with that SPV to be the developer.

There may be a clear profit-share agreement based on the original forecast and you may have to support this with a set of personal guarantees, assuring the funder their proportion of feasibility profits. Once the development has been completed, there will be a profit-share based on actual realised profits. Any losses would be typically supported by yourself as the development partner. Rates vary but can be circa 10-14% and as always, due diligence should be undertaken in looking at this specialist model. However, for those who have no access to current capital in ensuring their development gets funded, this can be a viable option to explore.

Development finance

Senior debt would generally be the most popular form of commercial and development finance and would take the first charge on the property asset. Additional to senior debt, there is the possibility of mezzanine finance. Mezzanine finance is particularly specialised and would sit in ranking behind senior debt. See the table below for how the types of funding can interact:

Finance	Ranking	Security	LTC	Sum	Return	Fxd/Var
Senior Debt	Returned 1st	1st charge	70-80%	750,000	4-10%	Fixed
Mezzanine	Returned 2nd	2nd charge	10-20%	150,000	14-20%+	Fixed
Equity	Returned 3rd	Shareholder	10-20%	100,000	Profit	Variable
Profit	Returned 4th	nil	n/a	200,000	n/a	Variable
			100%	£1,200,000		

(Left margin: Risk Increase — Right margin: Returns Increase)

Your potential funder will generally work on two lending base decisions - percentage loan-to-cost (LTC) and percentage loan to gross development value (LTGDV).

Your development project will generally be funded by two or possibly three tranches of funding:

1. Senior debt - this is the most secure debt of all

2. Mezzanine finance - not always required

3. Private capital or equity capital

The senior debt funding will always require a first security charge on the property, almost certainly a debenture on the company and also personal guarantees from the directors of the company. We will consider personal guarantees a little later on in this chapter. They rank first in order of security and therefore, the senior debt will be the first to be paid back. As a consequence of their relatively low risk profile, the returns tend to be somewhat lower than other funding routes and can be in the region of 4% to 10% per annum on a fixed basis. Mezzanine finance would always sit behind the first charge of senior debt so they would potentially take a second charge on the property should senior debt allow that.

Note, not all senior debt providers will allow a second charge and therefore, a mezzanine finance option might not be possible unless you consider an alternative senior debt provider.

Mezzanine finance would be returned after senior debt has been repaid. The loan-to-cost would typically be much less than senior debt and in the aggregate, a mezzanine provider would generally not top up senior debt to an overall funding level of more than

85% to 90%. For example, if a senior debt provider was lending at 70%, then mezzanine would probably not provide any more than 15% to 20%. The returns for mezzanine funders is higher, given that their risk profile is also higher and can be between 12% to 25% on a fixed return basis.

The third area of funding is equity and private capital. This will rank third place behind senior debt and mezzanine. Generally, the security charge would be a shareholding in the company, although if there is an absence of mezzanine funding, it may be possible for a second charge to be available on the property. This again depends on whether the senior debt provider will allow this. The private capital equity requirement, typically, would be somewhere between 10% to 25% and their returns would be on a proportion of profits basis typically and therefore, are at a variable and not a fixed rate.

The example table above demonstrates a £1,200,000 GDV development funding with senior debt, mezzanine and private capital to provide an illustration of how risk and return profiling works with your funding structure.

Funders security

Let us consider other elements of the security package that your commercial and development funders may also require. As we have discussed before, the senior debt provider will require:

1. First charge on the property at Land Registry. This first charge will enable the funder to recover their loan should the company default in any way on its obligations. This is a relatively rare occurrence, but does happen and you should be absolutely aware that this is an asset-based security loan.

2. Debenture on the company. A debenture is a charge on the company itself and all assets that reside within. If acquiring the property in a special-purpose vehicle (SPV), (limited company or LLP) established purely for this development, then it may be of only passing concern to us. However, should you be developing a second asset in an existing company, then debentures can become

complicated through cross-collateralisation challenges with other funders.

3. Personal guarantees. Personal guarantees should be taken seriously, and you will be required to take advice. Please allow time for this to happen as the funder may request that you seek advice from an independent solicitor and formally documented. This is referred to as Independent Legal Advice (ILA). It will probably come as no surprise that you will have to bear the cost of this independent solicitor giving you advice, certifying to the lender that this has been undertaken and that you signed the personal guarantee knowing exactly what you signed.

Personal Guarantees

Personal guarantees are there as the ultimate level of backstop security. What the funders do not want is you throwing the keys across the table at them and handing over the property if life gets a little bit hard!

The ultimate sanction is that funders can take recourse against your personal assets in the event of a default. It is not that they wish to turf your family out onto the street, claim your property and your personal assets it's more that they wish to hold your feet to the fire and feel confident that you will back the project and see it through to conclusion throughout all the challenges and obstacles that may present themselves, until they get their capital repaid. Personal guarantees are, or will almost certainly be, a requirement for you. You will need to get comfortable with them - it is a mind-set. Please talk to your commercial broker to ensure you understand what is likely to be required and that you consult your solicitor to get best advice.

"What the funders do not want is you throwing the keys across the table at them, and handing over the property if life gets a little bit hard!"

The level that you would be expected to guarantee would not represent the entire cost of the project – actually somewhere between 20-30% of the senior debt. If there are more than one of you as directors of the SPV, it is likely that you will all need to be prepared to sign guarantees on a 'joint and severally liable' basis. Bear in mind that this would mean that in the event of a failure, the funder could seek recourse from any of the personally guaranteeing parties in an order of their choosing.

The shareholder agreement for your new company is where you would be prescriptive between shareholders on what would happen in the event of a single guaranteeing director being pursued by the funder under the guarantee, therefore becoming liable and how then the others would be equally liable and the process that that takes to ensure equitability.

Quite often commercial and development funders are smaller than main high street banks, although main high street banks will lend on this basis too. It is always good to meet your development funder and also your commercial broker. Relationships are important and personal contact can convey a level of confidence and reassurance, both ways, where documentation sometimes cannot. A strong recommendation would be to create relationships and this will prove invaluable in navigating the various challenges and hurdles that you will need to overcome throughout the course of your project.

Your commercial and development finance partner understands that not everything goes according to plan all the time, but they will seek confidence and assurance from your ability to communicate regularly, openly, and honestly and keep them up to speed on problems.

Where personal guarantees have been triggered, invariably it has been where developers have buried their heads at the sight of problems and not discussed openly with funders. Funders can help provide solutions, so please bring them in as part of your team and certainly do not remain silent on any issues or ignore them.

Important: Ensure that you do not assume that once the senior debt is paid back and all obligations fulfilled, that the guarantees automatically fall away. You should have a housekeeping function that records all your guarantees that you enter into and record the execution of Deed of Releases for each one as you exit. This will be something that your solicitor will handle with the lenders solicitor and you should ensure that you have a sum of money allocated for the cost of confirming and signing the deed of release. Typically, this might be between £50 - £150 per guarantor being released. Therefore, if you have 4 directors all providing guarantees on a joint and severally liable basis then the costs would be £200 - £600.

The same would also apply in preparing and signing a deed of release for debentures held on the company, again usually with your senior debt lender.

Security Charges

Security charges are many and varied, however they are an essential consideration in almost all forms of funding. Here are a few forms of security that are frequently utilised within investment and funding circles:

1. 1st charge – on a property registered at Land Registry.

2. 2nd charge – on a property registered at Land Registry. This form of charge will almost certainly require approval of the 1st charge lender (who is at no obligation to allow a 2nd charge).

3. Restriction / RX1 – a form of security charge where the beneficiary cannot invoke action but it provides a restriction on the sale of the property until lifted. This may frequently be held on an unencumbered property as security against a loan.

4. Shareholding – security in the form of a shareholding (often in the SPV) which can be presented in the form of differing share classes and subject to conditions held within the shareholder agreement.

5. Deed of Trust – a legally binding agreement registering the financial arrangements between joint owners of a property as well as other parties who may have an active financial interest in the property. The agreement is generally made at the time of purchasing the property and is designed to clarify exactly what happens to all

interested parties financial interests in the future, thus minimising disputes.

6. Debentures – this is frequently requested by the 1st charge lender on an SPV in addition to its usual 1st charge security. The debenture gives the funder security on all other assets held by the company.

7. Floating charges – generally available only to companies and is usually an equitable charge on all the company's assets, both present and future. This may also include a charge on a specific type of asset such as stock, vehicles or machinery.

8. Personal Guarantee – frequently commercial funding is conditional on the directors of the company entering into personal guarantees. In entering into this form of guarantee the lender may well demand Independent Legal Advice (ILA) be taken from a separate solicitor to ensure that an audit trail can be achieved, clarifying that the director entered into the guarantee on an 'eyes wide open' basis and was fully aware of the implications of what they were signing. ILA's can be £200-£400 per director so make sure you budget for this in your cost plan.

9. Parent Company Guarantee – This form is usually reserved for corporate transactions or where you have multiple SPVs and hold your interests in a holding company with a certain holding of assets of value. It is worth considering this more fully when presented with this demand as this does extend the security package requested from the lender to well beyond the boundaries of a 1st charge, debenture and personal guarantees.

It is worthy of note that one party has an even greater level of security than any of the other security charges mentioned above – and that is HMRC. Hence you may well find your 1st charge funder being very specific about the

"one party has an even greater level of security than any of the other security charges mentioned above – and that is HMRC"

professional compliance, governance, fiduciary duties and probity levels that you as a company director operate your company to. Your failure to comply with HMRC obligations could be one of very few events that could trump their security package of 1st charge and debenture and leave them picking the bones out of the business after a tax failure and following HMRC recovery proceedings.

Private Investment

The reality of any development is that private capital is going to be a requirement for it to proceed.

As we have seen earlier, senior debt will typically loan up to 70-80% of the costs of the development and the introduction of mezzanine would take the total loan up to a maximum of 85-90%, leaving somewhere between 10-25% of your development overall cost to find (depending on funding structure) from other sources.

At this stage we need to look carefully again at the security charges.

We know that the senior debt funder will always require 1st charge on the property purchase. If we deploy a separate commercial funder for the development funding side i.e. the construction/ refurbishment phase, then they will also require a 1st charge. Therefore, it is almost always going to be the case where the overall commercial funding of the purchase and the development phase would be via a single senior debt provider who would have access to that all important 1st charge.

It may be possible to structure funding to enable private investment to secure the building or land, in cash, with no requirement for a 1st charge, therefore leaving optimum senior debt on the development facility.

This may occur when the property is already owned on an unencumbered basis, or when a private investor has funds to make the purchase in cash and accepts a level of security other than a 1st charge on this property.

Generally though, private investor capital of circa 10-25% of the development costs is required to ensure the development can proceed.

Where can these funds be found? Well, from a variety of places, however it must be made very clear at this stage that you should seek advice and ensure that you are familiar with what is required to undertake this properly and in a compliant manner as the Financial Conduct Authority (FCA) regulates this area.

Potential sources of private funds include:

- Yourself
- Directors of the company
- Partners of the LLP
- Shareholders of the company
- Sophisticated private investors
- Professional investors
- High net-worth individuals (HNWI)
- Ultra-high net-worth individuals (UHNWI)
- Pension funds via a SSAS or SIPP
- Institutional funds
- Company loan
- Overseas funding

Whatever the source of the funds, you must ensure that you comply fully with the following golden rules:

1. Compliance with FCA Policy Statement 13/3 Restrictions on the retail distribution of unregulated collective investment schemes and close substitutes.
2. Make sure your commercial broker is fully aware and discloses your origination of private funds to your commercial funder.
3. Seek independent tax, legal and accounting advice at all stages.

"ensure you remain fully compliant with the FCA PS13/3 governance requirements"

This book does not give advice on how to raise funds; separate legal and compliance advice must always be taken before engaging in any conversations remotely around this subject to ensure you remain fully compliant with the FCA PS13/3 governance requirements. Remember that this is for your protection as well as that of the potential investor.

Retail investor(s)	A retail investor is a person who invests in their capacity as a retail client – that is, a client who is neither a professional client nor an eligible counterparty. Professional clients and eligible counterparties are defined in COBS 3 and, generally speaking, are institutional clients and individuals who invest by way of business. In this paper we distinguish between three types of retail customer:
	(i) Sophisticated investor(s)
	Retail clients meeting the criteria for categorisation as sophisticated investors under any of the sophisticated investor exemptions in the PCIS Order, the FPO or in our rules. These are retail clients with extensive investment experience and knowledge of complex instruments, who are better able to understand and evaluate the risks and potential rewards of unusual, complex and/or illiquid investments such as NMPIs.
	(ii) High net worth individual(s)
	Retail clients meeting the criteria for categorisation as high net worth individuals under any of the high net worth investor exemptions in the PCIS Order, the FPO or in our rules. Among the criteria are having an annual income of more than £100,000 or having investable net assets of more than £250,000. These criteria are subject to review and may be updated in future.
	(iii) Ordinary retail investor(s)
	In this Policy Statement we use the term 'ordinary retail investor' to refer to retail clients who are neither sophisticated investors nor high net worth individuals. These are the investors of ordinary means and experience who make up the vast majority of the retail market in the UK. As discussed in a 2012 consultation paper by the International Organization of Securities Commissions (IOSCO), such investors face difficulty understanding the terms and features of complex financial products.[1] Such investors are at particular risk in relation to inappropriate promotion of non-mainstream pooled investments.

https://www.fca.org.uk/publication/policy/ps13-03.pdf

Typically, your funding can come from two main routes:

1. A loan agreement – a fixed return on capital loaned for a defined period of time. As an example the following may be considered within the detailed agreement:

   a. Total value of loan

   b. Timing of loan – when loan is made

   c. Duration of the loan

   d. Security on the loan

   e. Return on the loan – generally a fixed interest rate

   f. Terms of interest repayment – monthly, annually or rolled up at end of term

   g. Default clause – what happens in the event of failure to meet intended repayment timescales

Risk appetite: loan agreements work in a multitude of ways. However, they can typically be considered appropriate for parties who have little interest or appetite for risks associated with a development and are more comfortable with a fixed rate of return for a duration.

Always use a solicitor for this transaction for compliance, professionalism and clarity. Using the solicitor's client account can be a very independent method of managing the timing of funds and security transfer once all parties are happy to proceed, in a very similar way to how the day of legal completion on a property purchase happens.

2. Private Capital/Equity – the investor provides capital into the SPV to fund the development in return for a proportion of the profits at the predefined exit of the development. Elements would include:

   a. Total value of injected capital

   b. Security – typically shareholding, however can include 2nd charge, RX1, security on other assets if available or deed of trust etc

   c. Basis of a Return - % share of net profits of SPV

   d. Tax considerations

e. Timing of capital injected and capital sum repaid

Once you have a carefully screened an FCA PS 13/3 compliant short list of sophisticated and high net worth individuals, you should consider how you professionally present the opportunity to them.

An Investment Memorandum is the favoured route of many developers. This professionally produced document may include the following areas to introduce your sophisticated investors to the opportunity:

- Summary of the opportunity
- High level economics of the development – GDV, Costs, Anticipated Profit and ROCE
- About us – explain who you are and your experience etc
- Investor opportunity – the details of what, when, how long, security and returns
- Location and local setting of the development
- Photos – current, as well as any visualisations of the final product if available
- Planning position – status and plan
- Layouts
- Design and positioning of the end product
- Gross Development Value - Build up in summary of GDV
- High level overall economics of the development
- Source of funding
- Timeline/milestones
- Previous track record

Much of the background information on you, your company and your track record will have been covered in your initial meetings once you have established a rapport with your sophisticated private investors. However, they may have any number of possible enquiries at any particular time so a brief resume summary is always useful.

How long should this document be? Well, the short answer is as long as it needs to be to succinctly and accurately convey the high level appraisal of the development opportunity to the sophisticated investor. Around 12-16 pages would be an average which can be digested in a 5-10 minute initial review.

You should be mindful that this is an initial document and should be able to be quickly and readily absorbed, to ascertain interest. Too long and the simplicity of the opportunity will be lost – too short and credibility may be lost.

It is also worthy of note that different people learn and absorb information in different ways and a few different approaches to bear in mind might include the following when considering your investors:

- Visual – prefer to see information and visualise
- Auditory – prefer to hear information rather than read about it so may wish to have a call or meet up to discuss
- Reading/writing – prefer to read, analyse and see data
- Kinaesthetic – prefer a hands on experiential basis and may wish to visit the site

The clear message here is to balance the needs of the sophisticated investor and their preferred method of reviewing opportunities.

A Revolution in Funding – Synergy Funding

Incredibly exciting for me is Synergy Funding transforming how we fund developments for developers and also how we enable investors the opportunity to invest their capital.

This is a powerful and collaborative platform that enables the union between investor and developer with confidence and assurance.

The definition described by the Cambridge Dictionary:

Synergy: The combined power of a group of things when they are working together that is greater than the total power achieved by each working separately

"Synergy Funding transforming how we fund developments for developers"

To find out more about how Synergy Funding can help your developments be funded through collaborative funding "BY developers, FOR developers", then visit us at www.synergyfunding.co.uk

My Personal SSAS Funding journey

> *I have looked in the mirror every morning and asked myself: 'If today were the last day of my life, would I want to do what I am about to do today?' And whenever the answer has been 'No' for too many days in a row, I know I need to change something - Steve Jobs*

As part of my 26-year corporate career I had been a pension contributor since day one of leaving polytechnic back in 1992. In reality, while I was a chairman, managing director, director or non-executive director I was probably still in the 99% of the population who received their pension statements once a year, looked rather unimpressed at them for a few seconds and promptly hoped the performance might improve the next year – hardly an active participant in the day-to-day direction of one of my largest 'bank accounts'!

That summarised my annual contribution to my pension management strategy for 26 years, outsourcing the pension contributions to my payroll colleagues and the 'active' management to a number of stakeholder/final salary pension scheme providers, who probably charged me substantial fees for the privilege.

The decision to retire from corporate life while still in my mid-40's was enshrined on the principle of wanting to spend more time with my family and friends, to live life on my own terms and to build a multi-generational legacy for my children based on solid principles of entrepreneurship.

The final 'severing of the umbilical cord' of corporate life was to consider my options on my pensions that I had accumulated over the years. I was no longer happy to allow others to dictate and control my wealth and direction, hence I set about considering the options available for taking control of my pensions.

I considered the following two options:

Self-Invested Personal Pension (SIPP)

A Self-Invested Personal Pension (SIPP) is the name given to a type of UK government-approved personal pension scheme, which allows individuals to make their own investment decisions from a range of investments approved by HM Revenue and Customs (HMRC), making them highly tax efficient.

Investors may make choices about what assets are bought, leased or sold and decide when those assets are acquired or disposed of, subject to the agreement of the SIPP provider.

All assets are permitted by HMRC, however some will be subject to tax charges. The assets that are not subject to a tax charge are:

- Stocks and shares listed on a recognised exchange
- Futures and options traded on a recognised futures exchange
- Authorised UK unit trusts and open-ended investment companies and other UCITS funds
- Unauthorised unit trusts that do not invest in residential property
- Unlisted shares
- Investment trusts subject to FCA regulation
- Unitised insurance funds from EU insurers and IPAs
- Deposits and deposit interests
- Commercial property (including hotel rooms)
- Ground rents (as long as they do not contain any element of residential property).
- Traded endowments policies
- Derivatives products such as a contract for difference (CFD)
- Gold bullion, which is specifically allowed for in legislation, provided it is 'investment grade'.

Investments typically not permitted by SIPP providers due to significant tax penalties include:

- Assets such as vintage cars, wine, stamps, watches and art
- Residential property

Small Self-Administered Scheme (SSAS)

Small Self-Administered Scheme (SSAS) is a trust based Pension Scheme and is usually established by directors of a limited company referred to as a 'sponsoring' company for specific employees and/ or shareholders of the company.

The sponsoring employer can also pay contributions to the scheme and may obtain tax relief on the contributions.

SSAS Trusts are registered with HMRC and can benefit from tax-exempt status, with all investments made free of Capital Gains Tax and contributions to the SSAS will receive tax-relief. Basic rate tax relief can be claimed by the SSAS itself.and any higher rate tax would be claimed through the member's tax return.

"controlling a hugely powerful multi-generational wealth creation vehicle"

The Trustees may wish to appoint a professional company to assist with the management of the scheme. This company may operate as a SSAS Practitioner or as the Scheme Administrator. They both carry out the tax returns and other such submissions to HMRC and the Regulator. If the scheme returns are not correctly undertaken a penalty can be assessed against the trustees of the pension scheme.

A SSAS is suited to groups of individuals who run common businesses and wish to have complete control over the pension fund. The costs per member are usually lower than using individual SIPPs to pool funds to purchase commercial property. SIPPs do not have the facility to loan funds to associated or un-associated employers. There is no requirement for a professional to be appointed to the scheme, but the rules are complex and may well prove difficult for individuals without experience running SSAS pensions.

The investments allowable for a SSAS are very similar to a SIPP. The Trustees of the SSAS may make choices about what assets are bought, leased or sold and decide when those assets are acquired or disposed of, subject to the unanimous agreement of all trustees.

After some deliberation it quickly became clear that the unregulated SSAS route allowed me the flexibility, control and accountability that I craved. This would help enable financial independence and security, in creating my own personal economy, particularly on a multi-generational basis.

Once the decision was made to go forward with a transfer we moved rapidly into the set-up and transfer phase – how hard could that be? Apparently you "can't have a baby without the labour pains" springs to mind and so it turned out!

Our submission to HMRC was held up in a random audit which delayed proceedings by seven months and the transfer process took longer than anticipated, due to highly uncooperative pension providers. However, with constant monitoring and chasing we eventually got there and my wife and I, along with two great friends, Nigel and Annette, became fellow trustees of our very own SSAS – a very proud moment after all that effort. However, it was the sense of freedom and control from the corporate machine and now controlling a hugely powerful multi-generational wealth creation vehicle that provided the most satisfaction.

I want to share something hugely personal with you at this stage which will forever resonate with deep sadness and leave a void in our lives. As I was exiting corporate life and contemplating the next steps in our long-term pension strategy, friends Nigel Greene and Peter Abbott were also contemplating this strategy and we ultimately decided to become Trustees together in our own SSAS.

Within a year of leaving corporate life and while still in his early 50s, Pete sadly passed away from a heart attack leaving his wife and three children, the youngest of whom was only two years old. In what was meant to be a defining and exhilarating time in his life, fate cruelly denied Pete and his loved ones that joy, leaving a void that will be eternal.

"a wealth legacy for future generations but also enables us to nurture the custodianship of that legacy in our youngsters"

Pete's set-up process

and pension transfer had not completed into the newly formed SSAS at the time of his passing and with devastating clarity, his life-long pension fund value was reduced on his passing by circa 50%.

There is a large portion of the population I suspect who live blissfully unaware that most pensions will take a huge reduction on the pension valuation (up to 50%) as the proceeds are passed to their beneficiaries.

Once pensions have been transferred into a SSAS, however, they are protected from Inheritance Tax and the Trusteeship can be transferred to the next generation.

This now forms a very important criterion for our SSAS moving forward. Not only does it create a wealth legacy for future generations but also enables us to nurture the custodianship of that legacy in our youngsters - Young Entrepreneurship live in action!

Pete taught me many things in the two decades that we were the best of friends and true to his most generous form, Pete continued to share and guide after his passing.

I miss you my friend.

And so the plans for our SSAS? Well it will be no surprise to those that know Nigel and I that these plans are significant, long term and will establish a bow wave of great value through serious compounding over many years to come.

Several key aspects include:

- To enable our SSAS philosophy to become part of our foundation learning platform for our family of young entrepreneurs – a true incubator of talent and business acumen.
- To establish a large portfolio of high-yielding commercial property assets.
- In creating commercial assets, establish further opportunities for adding value through conversion and enhancements .
- Use leverage to grow the Fund value exponentially over many years.
- Become 'black belts' in the Trust's management, opportunity seeking, value creation and risk management, compliance and governance associated with being a Trustee.
- Forge strong collaboration and synergy with other trustees and developers.

As the above demonstrates, our approach will certainly be an active one which will serve our strategic goals admirably. However, it is important for me to explain how this relates to our Time – our most precious commodity.

It would be true to say that being a Trustee could be a full-time role if you wanted it to be. Our Trust sits harmoniously and synergistically with our other business interests and the adage of "work hard to create the asset and then let the asset work hard for you" could not be more appropriate for our SSAS. We are clear that preservation of our time is paramount and hence we are carefully selecting assets which enable us to create an active engagement with minimal time required.

This would equally be true for our SSAS funding which will include:

- Cash purchases
- Loan backs

- Business loans
- Bank leverage
- Other SSAS collaboration

Our desired funding will take into account the risk v reward dynamics of what funding is required, how it is optimised and when it is engaged.

A good example of this would be the funding of a commercial to residential development. A SSAS cannot own residential assets, hence developing a conversion to residential scheme would require selling the end product prior to it becoming residential through its certificate of habitation/occupancy.

In effect, this requires selling and financing an incomplete asset, which creates a number of concerns and complexities for funders. For us as developers, it creates risk and uncertainty.

So what is our approach? We are fairly conservative and not arbitrary risk takers, choosing to select routes based on assured outcomes where possible. We prefer to undertake any conversion scheme in its own SPV if the strategy is to develop, sell and possibly develop in a property company (often referred to as a Prop Co) if the strategy is Hold, depending on the asset class mix.

Pause for thought - Creating a roadmap to assets certainty

Creating a roadmap to assets certainty has always been pivotal through my 26-year corporate and entrepreneurial career, operating global infrastructure businesses and deploying US $3bn of mission-critical infrastructure across four continents and 16 countries.

Over this time, I have learned many lessons along the way which are extremely relevant to the life of a property investor and developer.

Our Team was one of the very early adopters of PAS55, now ISO 55000 Standards for Asset Management which enabled us to consider every stage of the asset's lifecycle - this included property, engineering assets, power stations, data centres and water infrastructure etc. While many lessons in this complex, yet essential management system, were experienced whilst operating projects often in the US $100m+ range, the following seven lessons stand out as a solid start to understanding how to create a roadmap to maximising the certainty of the performance of the asset:

1. Start with the end in mind - but whose end and whose mind?

Is it the Funder, JV partner, Developer, Landowner, Local authority, Off-taker/purchaser, Tenant/leases Owner Operatives and the list goes on. Watch and listen to all sides of any negotiation and business case before pitching your angle. It is surprising how often other people's ideas can, if integrated with yours, create a more robust and mutually beneficial return. Proactive and also reactive negotiations (when crisis situation is experienced and emotions are running high) will benefit immensely with this approach and enable a win:win to be identified, if at all possible.

2. Protecting the cash flow/income stream is critical

Almost all commercial business/asset valuations are based on cash flow, income and profit being solidly underpinned and demonstrable. Experience shows that for increasingly complex business models, diversity of income exist and sources may not be unrelated, hence thorough due diligence and testing is required to ensure robustness of business plan assumptions minimising concentration risk and successful realisation of results.

3. Manage your costs with a passion

This sounds obvious but what you spend your precious capital on and how you spend it, could significantly affect your assets operation and therefore the cash flows that underpin your businesses valuation. Examine the cost/benefit of each part of your investment. Many of you know that Formula 1 has been a passion of mine for 20 years now and it was the unique Frank Williams of the Williams F1 Team who is famed for whenever anyone presented him an order/contract/cheque/idea, he would demand "How does this make the car go faster?". Now there is a leader and a team with a singularly focused and recognised objective.

4. Reliability is your assets backbone

Frank Williams makes a poignant statement in our last point and it won't be lost on him, that speed does not equal competitiveness, as reliability must be added into that equation. Reliability is not about pure maintenance (although this is incredibly important too), it is designed into the asset in the same way Health and Safety is, through The Construction (Design and Management) Regulations which effects now almost all construction projects.

Mike Hawthorn of motorsport fame once said that "If I can drive it home afterwards it was over-designed". Mike died on his way home in a car accident. We must think of the full asset cycle.

5. Establish highly systemised operations

Human error has usually been close to the top of categories of cause of failure - minimise this from the outset. I have witnessed at first hand many design flaws, system errors, losses of power, fibre connectivity breaks, reduction in resilience in all kinds of infrastructure. Yet inevitably, when a detailed Root Cause Analysis (RCA) has been conducted, it is human error through poor decision making, inappropriate design, budget constraints, operating error, lack of proper training, which contributed significantly to the loss occurring.

Your ability to effectively audit your business and operations will pay a handsome return for you - don't miss this stage out with the assumption that all is well; make sure it is proven to yourself and your team regularly.

6. Plan for the right outcome for all stakeholders to create shared value

Too often I have witnessed the 'bayoneting the wounded and robbing the bodies' approach to profiteering. When you truly operate in all stakeholders' interests you can see all party's values, efforts, contribution and the pleasure of collaboration and fulfilment become a core criterion for all. The creation of shared value can be achieved if we open our eyes to the wider stakeholders as positive contribution and societal impactfulness.

7. Evergreen asset

Time = Money. A fit-for-purpose design of an asset, with corrective, preventative and predictive maintenance embedded at a detailed level will gain the optimum utilisation of the asset and maximum 'up time' or time in service creating the desired revenue.

The evergreen element is hugely important to enable response and adaptation to the external environment - factors affecting the asset and out of your control (although frequently predictable if attention is paid in the right areas) such as government subsidy changes, economic environment, interest rates, weather, climate change (if the asset has a long lifetime), competition, legislations environmental sustainability etc. In a simple word: Anticipation.

I hope these seven key lessons from my Asset Management background will highlight and reinforce to you the critical importance and connective relationship between the secure and optimised longevity of an asset, its operating systems and underpinning of its economic equation.

8. Economics

Attitude is a little thing that makes a big difference
— Winston Churchill

Every element of the development is enshrined in the economic evaluation of the product, market, process, systems, funding and deliverables at every stage. The economics of the development enables us to quantify everything so that we can set goals, value risk and reward, measure contribution, decipher risk, enable audit and define outcomes.

Risk

A core theme that I trust is emerging for you throughout this book is that of Bank Grade Due Diligence which we refer to regularly and you should enshrine in your day to day processes.

A term from corporate banking which you will need to be aware of and consider is 'Concentration Risk'.

Concentration risk from a bank's perspective is, in basic terms, not putting all your eggs in one basket. A bank would typically not wish to expose their loan book to a risk level over and above certain preset criteria that would be administered by the team and approved through the Credit Risk process.

In considering concentration risk on a broader scale, we can adopt the due diligence that the bank use towards us on a wider context:

a. The Bank – looking to limit their risk by not being over exposed in certain scenarios.

b. Private Investors – may wish to diversify their investments across multiple developments and/or developers, with similar or further diverse investment criteria.

c. Area – is there enough demand in the area for the number of units planned?

d. Planners – is your development in line with the densification and type of development envisaged by the Local Planning Authority?

e. You – are your business or development interests too exposed in a particular area?

Note: just because the parameters have been exceeded in some of the areas above, does not necessarily mean that another developer, funder, property type or investor would not benefit from that strategy. We should always be mindful of having an open mind to multiple exit route options.

Tax

To many, tax is one of those areas that is a black art and one firmly in the camp of the accountants at the end of each tax year. In business, which remember that is what you are in as a developer, tax is the difference between working hard and working smart.

It is extremely easy to become so focused on the development in physical terms, caught up in the hype and excitement of what your newly found building will become, that you do not pay enough attention to your legal and tax structuring. Careful attention at the very start of your venture and thorough planning, with sound advice, will provide you the following benefits:

> **"know the VAT position before starting your development and not after"**

- Ensuring control and compliance
- Optimising your development returns
- Managing shareholder expectations and minimising surprises
- Enabling reliable forecasting
- Managing risk in advance rather than fire fighting
- Allowing you to sleep easy at night – don't underestimate this!

There is no substitute for proper advice, so make sure you have a great accountant and tax advisor as part of your professional team.

It is perfectly possible for your accountant to be your tax advisor, they can be from the same company, with or without 'Chinese walls'. However, not all accountants may be specialised in the areas of tax you require. You probably wouldn't be too keen to have a heart surgeon operate on your eyes, so careful selection of the correct type of specialist to serve your intended strategy is essential!

Value Added Tax

Value Added Tax (VAT) is a very complex subject and subject to specialist rules, however the basic principles we have highlighted consistently in this book will stand you in great stead to make informed decisions.

- Use a specialist tax advisor and accountant
- Work with them to assess your strategy AND your individual development deployment
- Start with the end in mind

- Remain compliant at all times

VAT on property is one of the most complicated areas of tax and one where you will need to know the VAT position before starting your development and not after.

One of the key questions to ask is: is the property domestic or commercial?

Below is a summary of the highlights of some important elements of VAT, but you must ensure that you get specialist advice from your accountant on the most current and relevant advice for your business and/or development.

Below is a summary of various property development permutations which are meant as a guide:

Domestic – Buying and Selling

Buying - No VAT

Renting - No VAT

Selling - New build – 0% VAT

Selling - Second hand – Exempt from VAT

Domestic – Building and renovation work

New Build - Builders charge 0% VAT – Other fees 20% - All recoverable if built to sell - non recoverable if built to rent

Renovation/refurb - Occupied in the 2 years before the work starts – All bought in goods and services 20% VAT – Non recoverable

Renovation/refurb - Not occupied in the 2 years before the work starts - Builders charge 5% VAT – Other fees 20% - Non recoverable

Renovation/refurb - Not occupied in the 10 years before the work starts - Builders charge 5% VAT – Other fees 20% - Renovated for sale – All VAT recoverable – Renovated for rent – No VAT recoverable.

Commercial - Buying and Selling

Buying - less than 3 years old – VAT 20%

Selling - less than 3 years old – VAT 20%

Buying - more than 3 years old – VAT exempt unless the seller has opted to tax – then 20%

Selling - more than 3 years old – VAT exempt unless the seller opts to tax – then 20%

Rented – VAT exempt unless the seller has opted to tax – then 20%

Building and renovation work – All 20%

New build for sale – All VAT recoverable

New build for rent – No VAT recoverable unless the landlord opts to tax and charges VAT on the rent.

Second hand (more than 3 years old) - For sale - No VAT recoverable unless the landlord opts to tax and charges VAT on the sale.

For rent - No VAT recoverable unless the landlord opts to tax and charges VAT on the rent.

Conversions - Commercial to domestic

Converted for sale – 0% VAT

Converted for rent – Exempt from VAT

Builders charge 5% VAT – Other fees 20% - All recoverable if built to sell – non recoverable if built to rent

Conversions - Domestic - changing the number of dwelling units within an existing building

Sale or rent - Exempt from VAT

Builders charge 5% VAT – Other fees 20% - Non recoverable

Special rules for nursing homes, student accommodation and charity buildings.

Always seek expert advice.

VAT on Commercial property

One of the fundamental differences between commercial property and residential property is VAT. A commercial property may well be elected for VAT and hence at the prevailing current rate of 20% you would be paying 20% VAT on the purchase price.

Example:

Purchase price	£1,250,000
VAT	£250,000

Overall cost of purchase   £1,500,000

Clearly being misinformed or making an error in your VAT strategy can lead to some unwelcome surprises.

If the intention is to acquire a commercial property and convert to apartments, then it may be possible to disapply VAT through an HMRC VAT 1614D form. This form will need to be run through your solicitor and accountant, prior to purchase, as well as the selling vendor of the property and once executed will mean zero VAT would apply on the purchase price.

Example:

Purchase price: £1,250,000

VAT   £0 (with 1614D)

Overall cost of purchase: £1,250,000

Do be aware that this only applies to commercial to residential elements of the building. So, for example if we have acquired a 'mixed use development' opportunity where the ground floor consisted of three retail units, with offices above and the intention was to retain the retail units in their current form and convert the upper offices to residential, then the following VAT might apply.

Example:

Area split

Retail   40%

Office to residential   60%

Purchase price   £1,250,000

Vat on Retail   £1,250,000x 40% x 20% = £100,000

VAT with 16140   £1,250,000 x 60% x 0% = £0

Total VAT   £100,000

Overall cost of purchase   £1,350,000

Capital Allowances

Capital allowances are a tax relief in lieu of depreciation and are claimed on the cost of plant and machinery existing within a commercial property.

They can significantly reduce tax liability, can sometimes result in a tax rebate and are therefore an important consideration in any property developer's tax planning. Specialist advice from a tax specialist(s) is again crucial in this area and interpreting the tax rules is essential. As an example, there is no definition of what constitutes plant or machinery in the taxes acts.

* It is part specified in Capital Allowances Act 2001 (CAA 2001)
* Confirmed in legal precedent – prior legal cases

It is possible to get tax relief on plant and machinery which can be defined broadly as:

* Heating
* Lighting
* Power Supplies
* Sanitary Ware and Kitchen installations
* Carpeting
* Air conditioning

You cannot get tax relief on the following categories of a building:

* Foundations
* Bricks and Walls
* Roof
* Flooring
* Drainage

The summary components of a capital allowances tax relief claim include:

* Capital allowances can only be claimed once in the lifetime of any property – establish if there has been a historical claim
* Allowances can be off set against any income stream
* Sideways Loss Relief depending on the structuring of your

group of companies

- Holiday lets, serviced accommodation, commercial properties and certain residential works
- Residential property generally is not allowable
- From 5% - 150% of your capital investment can qualify
- Can include purchase price of property and certain refurbishment costs
- HMRC say 96% of available allowances have NOT been claimed!

It is important for the developer to agree the plant value in the building, with the vendor, within two years of purchase:

- Fail and you get nothing
- Endeavour to agree as part of the sale negotiations
- If the vendor will not agree – potential for a Tax Tribunal
- It is a business cost in your accounts, reduces your 'taxable' profit and hence your tax.
- Only the 'owner' of the property can claim
- Parties that may claim include:

> You
>
> Your spouse
>
> Partnership
>
> Limited company you control

- Non-Dwelling premises only

A word of caution for you in this area. Whilst capital allowances can indeed be an incredibly powerful stimulus for your business as it is intended to be by HMRC, it is also an area where you will require specialist advice. You will require your accountant, a specialist capital allowances surveyor and possibly your solicitor to work closely together.

It is worth noting that you can outsource for advice but you cannot outsource decision making and the ultimate accountability that comes with that. I strongly suggest that you use your accountant, solicitor and capital allowances surveyor to test each others' opinions and advice to the point where maximum clarity is achieved before deploying this strategy. Failure to comply, or inaccurate use of the rules, will result in you and your business feeling the full weight of HMRC and their penalty process.

The legal entity that you are claiming capital allowances within can make a substantial difference in the tax efficiency of your strategy.

Certain legal entities are already highly tax efficient and therefore are unable to claim capital allowances. Two examples of this may include:

- Trusts
- Local Authorities/Government

Should your strategy and business be seeking the substantial benefits of capital allowances, you can certainly apply this knowledge when approaching and acquiring land and commercial property opportunities by understanding what legal entity the property is currently owned in which potentially could result in the most commercially beneficial advantage for you. A cautionary note would be to consider the lifetime of the ownership of the assets as previous owners could have claimed capital allowances and they can only be claimed ONCE.

Experience has generally shown that if your strategy is 'Buy, Develop, Sell' then the C3 use class apartments that you are creating would be held as 'stock' on the balance sheet in your SPV accounts, for a relatively short period of time and therefore would not be eligible under HMRC rules for capital allowances.

Should your strategy be 'Buy, Develop, Hold' then the apartments would be held as fixed assets on the balance sheet of your company and therefore capital allowances may well be something you should consider.

"consider the lifetime of the ownership of the assets"

Once again we see that the phrase 'start with the end in mind' will pay enormous dividends by ensuring you establish the correct structure and approach to your business interests. In identifying the type of property you are searching for and your intended purpose for that property, you will be able to incorporate the most appropriate advice from your professional team and ensure maximum efficiency and compliance over the term of your business interests.

There are numerous tax efficient allowances which you might consider with your specialist tax team, some of these include:

1. Capital Allowances – as discussed earlier in the chapter.

2. Enhanced Capital Allowances - The Enhanced Capital Allowance (ECA) energy scheme aims to encourage businesses to invest in certain energy saving technologies.

   The ECA energy scheme lets your business claim 100% first-year tax relief on investments in qualifying technologies and products. This means you can write off, i.e. deduct - the whole cost, or up to the published claim value, of buying the energy-saving product against your taxable profits in the year of purchase.

   ECA's bring forward tax relief, so that you can set it against profits from a period earlier than would otherwise be the case.

3. Land Remediation Relief - Land Remediation Relief is a relief from corporation tax only. It provides a deduction of 100%, plus an additional deduction of 50%, for qualifying expenditure incurred by companies in cleaning up land acquired from a third party in a contaminated state.

Land Remediation Relief can enable up to 150% tax relief under certain circumstances - it pays to be informed!

Land or buildings are in a contaminated state if there is contamination present as a result of industrial activity such that:

- It is causing relevant harm
- There is a serious possibility that it could cause relevant harm
- It is causing, or there is a serious possibility that it could cause, significant pollution in the groundwater, streams, rivers or coastal waters.

'Relevant harm' includes significant adverse impact on the health of humans, animals or damage to buildings that has a real impact on the way the building is used.

Qualifying expenditure includes the cost of establishing the level of contamination, removing the contamination or containing it so that the possibility of relevant harm is removed. There is, however, no relief if the remediation work is not carried out.

Land Remediation Relief is available for both capital and revenue expenditure. However, the company must elect, within two years of the end of the accounting period in which the expenditure is incurred, to treat qualifying capital expenditure as a deduction in computing taxable profits.

In addition to the deduction for the cost of the land remediation, the company can claim an additional deduction in computing its taxable profits. This additional deduction is 50% of the qualifying expenditure. A company can claim this additional deduction at any time within the general time limit for claims under Corporation Tax Self-Assessment. HMRC does not specify any particular form for the claim. A computation reflecting the claim and submitted in time is sufficient. The 50% additional relief is given in the same period as the actual expenditure is charged to the profit and loss account.

The Market

There has been much commentary by economists on the cycles of the UK property markets and how average property prices have traditionally increased by X% every 10 years. Of course there is much analysis and many variables that will affect this.

The timing of your investments in the market will probably be the most important factor to you, rather than how extrapolated growth curves over centuries have held the test of time!!

For example, if property prices in your region

"There are numerous tax efficient allowances which you might consider with your specialist tax team"

have doubled on average every 12 years over the past 100 years, that is probably of little comfort to you if over the past eight years property prices have flat-lined with no growth and predicted to only marginally grow in the next 5 years.

Equally, if a major infrastructure announcement such as the HS2 high speed railway programme or the Queen Elizabeth underground line is coming to your area, then property prices can spike dramatically in a very short period of time.

So what does this mean to us as developers? Well it is going to come down to a number of factors:

1. Know your product and how it sits within the market
2. Know the area that your product is going to be applied to
3. Do your bank grade due diligence on each property
4. Continuously monitor your area during the course of the development

As we know from the valuation process, no funder will take a view on where the market is going – only where it has been. Therefore, your assessment of potential should be firmly anchored in its base case model, by the historical comparable sold prices in the local area.

Pause for thought - Establishing Resilience

Much of my working life, whether running tens or hundreds of £millions of development infrastructure, operating and leading businesses, being a corporate trouble-shooter or serving our customers, has been based on resilience at a personal, team, operational and corporate level.

When failure happens, the engineering term for the 'review' is a Root Cause Analysis (RCA). Resilience of mission critical infrastructure is paramount - in today's 7 x 24 x 365 global world of business, even the five 9s principal of 99.999% resilience will not allow for the 0.001% chance of the lights going out on a business.

When you bear in mind much of our operations, supported vast bank trading floors, stock exchanges, global telecommunications and data centres, it is not hard to see why there is such huge focus on learning from failures to ensure that every possible scrap of information and learning is driven back into the very operational and strategic heart of the business, to improve for the future.

Many lessons from corporate applications can be drawn from life at the pinnacle of risk management on a global basis, for those entrepreneurs who embrace leading thinking with humility.

Two particular lessons I would like to share both involve people, in fact in almost every case we did RCA's on we found the most prevalent route cause was human error. Many of our systems had very specific locking and switching systems that eliminated human intervention, albeit by a single individual, but systems can fail at an operational level.

Failure of your supply chain: To leverage and grow a specialist supply chain that supports your growth can be one of the most powerful leverage tactics any business can deploy - but do be aware of the perils of overloading your supply chain. It is seldom that a contractor will turn work away and their great results on the last development may not guarantee equally great results on the next development.

Always gain fresh covenant and accounting checks, to see if the business remains healthy, check pipelines and current contracts for signs of stress in workload and always take up references from your supply chain clients - don't just take the ones you are given on paper; talk to people!! Having a contractor go bust is one of the most stressful times for any development/business.

Equipment failure: "Buy cheap, buy twice" as the old saying goes. Negotiate hard and fair on the price point. However, I would counsel against compromising on quality. Longer-term replacement costs, lifecycle and operational maintenance and availability of spares generally will outweigh initial savings in the long run.

My strong recommendation is to build resilience into every facet of your business, always having other options and resources potentially available should the worst-case scenarios start to show signs of coming to fruition.

9. Completion

The person who says it can't be done should not interrupt the person who is doing it
- Chinese proverb

Legal completion is the culmination of the acquisition of the property when the title of the property is in the possession of you or your individual legal entity.

An old phrase comes to mind – "It is easy if you say it quickly". To ensure we anticipate the operational and legal requirements at each stage of getting a development over the start line efficiently, we need to understand each of the moving parts of the process and how they interact with each other.

We refer to this as Transaction Project Management.

The four core elements for Transaction Project Management are:

1. Conveyancing
2. Legal entity
3. Commercial funding
4. Private investor funding

Conveyancing

This is the core area which your commercial solicitor will manage on your behalf. However, there will be areas which you will have already undertaken that you will need to take advice on as you proceed.

For instance, the offer letter. Seek advice from your commercial solicitor on the structuring of your offer letter. This may not be required on every single offer, but make sure your offer is based on solid ground, uses the correct legal terminology to keep you safe and ensures that the offer you are making is received with the credibility to enable confidence in acceptance of your offer.

Once your offer has been accepted, you will receive the sales memorandum from the commercial agent. There may be a substantial amount of information required and

"you are committed to be buying the property even if it subsequently burns to the ground, hence, you must insure it from the point of exchange"

you will need to instruct your solicitor to act on your behalf.

In order for your solicitor to be on board, you will need to complete a substantial amount of documentation. This 'Know Your Customer' (KYC) process will enable your solicitor to go through the legal process of determining, with accuracy and surety, who you are, that everything is above board, anti-money laundering checks are being carried out and nothing is left to chance.

The conveyancing process will go through each step, looking at searches, the route of payments, all the due diligences of instructions, making sure all surveys are complete and the legal titles are checked. There are a few areas which you will need to look at, in addition - you will need to make sure you insure the property from the point of exchange. At the point of exchange, you are committed to buying the property even if it subsequently burns to the ground, hence, you must insure it from the point of exchange. You should note that the insurance will need to have your senior debt funder noted as a beneficiary of the policy and also the sum insured for rebuild must be no lower than the value stated in the senior debt providers RICS Red Book Valuation report for the development.

Searches

Searches are a core element of our legal and conveyancing due diligence process and enable us to uncover important information about the property that may not be revealed by other means. If you are taking out commercial funding on the property, the commercial lender will insist that certain "standard" searches are carried out and probably a host of non-standard searches. The standard searches would include:

1. Local Search

This search looks into information held by the Local Authority relevant to the property and its use. This search should examine, for instance whether the road to the property is adopted or what planning permissions have been applied for.

Most of the information provided by this search is limited to the land/property inside the strict boundaries of the property you are buying. If you wish to obtain information on a particular issue relating to nearby property, you might instruct your own investigations or request a specialist search. An example might be the investigation of planning permission for construction or change of use on nearby land.

2. Environmental Search

The Environmental search is a desk top study for land contamination, flooding and other environmental issues, based on checking historical maps and other records and will not include any physical examination of the property.

There is often an expectation that the Local Search will show whether the property is included in the Local Authority Register of contaminated sites, however a negative result may mean the site has not been inspected and does not necessarily mean that there is no contamination.

The duty of care falls on you, as the developer, to make the appropriate searches and should additional certainty be required, then specialist searches may be instructed.

3. Water/Drainage Search

Water and drainage searches check fresh water supply and drainage provisions, however, do not address any flooding assessment.

There are various other additional searches that may be required to assess, on a more detailed basis, a full and proper title/security investigation, depending on the location of the property or other factors.

Specialist searches vary across the country with some areas not requiring certain searches as they are highly localised. However far better to discount the requirement than to have never considered a vital piece of potential due diligence in the first place. Ignorance is no excuse as they say!

These specialist searches might include:

a. Coal and Tin Mining Searches

A check for issues relating to underground mining which is

instructed where the property is in an area where one of these types of mining happens, or used to happen.

b. Utility Searches (Electricity/Gas/Telecommunications)

Searches to confirm the location of pipes and cables in the vicinity of the property through individually instructed enquiry searches to the various utility operators in that area.

c. Chancel Repair Search

Some properties, which are located on former rectorial land, may be liable to contribute to the cost of repairs to the chancel of a church. It is possible to carry out a search to check for this liability. If a potential risk is revealed by the search, it is possible to insure against the risk by payment of a one-off premium.

d. Radon Gas

Should the Local Search reveal that Radon is an issue in the area of the purchase property, an additional enquiry to the National Radiological Protection Board can be made to establish whether the property has been tested for Radon and if so, the results of the tests.

e. Commons Registration Search

A search to check whether any part of the property, or any access to it, is registered as Common Land.

f. Highway Search

A search to identify the precise extent of the adjoining roads/paths/verges which are adopted and maintainable at public expense. If the road is not adopted and is private, then rights of way are required and the cost of maintenance would normally fall to the owners of properties having such rights.

j. Plan Search

Should the aforementioned searches reveal information on the land surrounding the property being purchased, including planning permissions submitted and information about local amenities, then more detailed searches can be instructed to establish the purpose, extent and detail of those planned or considered developments.

h. Flood Risk Assessment

A flood search will provide a risk assessment for your property where flooding may be an issue. Some properties may become uninsurable owing to repeated floods and your insurers will want to understand the previous history of flooding in the property.

Commercial Property Standard Enquiries (CPSE)

An important part of the process which your solicitor will need your support on, are the Commercial Property Standard Enquiries (CPSE) which aim to standardise and speed up the process of commercial property conveyancing. CPSE was introduced in October 2002 and is divided into 5 sections:

CPSE 1 - covers all commercial property transactions:

- Freehold
- Leasehold
- Vacant
- Tenanted

Supplemental enquiries where:

- CPSE 2: property is sold subject to commercial tenancies.
- CPSE 3: lease of a property is being granted.
- CPSE 4: property is being sold is leasehold.
- CPSE 5: lease of a property is being surrendered.

Pre-contract enquiries can be time consuming and look cumbersome but replies to enquiries are an important source of information for a buyer.

At the start of most property transactions, a prospective buyer will raise enquiries about the property which it intends to acquire.

The onus is on the buyer to carry out a thorough review of the property and to identify any potential issues. In commercial transactions the Commercial Property Standard Enquiries, or CPSEs, are usually raised to help standardise the type of questions usually requested and information disclosed.

These are a comprehensive set of enquiries which help a buyer to understand the property and the interest that it is acquiring. A thorough set of replies can facilitate a speedy conclusion to a deal.

The seller is not under any duty to give replies but it is under a legal duty to disclose latent defects affecting the property. Examples of these include a right of way not obvious from a site inspection or noted in the deeds, rights of drainage and third party interests. Offering full replies helps to ensure that the seller has discharged its duty.

Transfer of Going Concern

When acquiring a property, at offer stage, one of the first question to ask is "What are we offering to buy?" This may sound strange as this book is all about commercial property conversions to residential apartments. However, primarily rather than purchasing a property, we may in fact be purchasing a company. This might be referred to as a Transfer of Going Concern (TOGC).

The level of due diligence surrounding a TOGC purchase, as opposed to a standard commercial property purchase can be significant as you will not only be acquiring the commercial property but also all the ongoing assets and liabilities of the business. Due diligence would need to be undertaken on the full set of accounts on the company and any outstanding claims etc, which will need to be particularly thorough.

As a consequence, you should expect that the legal costs of a TOGC acquisition will be more expensive in legal fees and the process will almost certainly take longer.

In certain circumstances special TOGC rules apply and the sale will not be treated as a supply for VAT purposes, so no VAT should be charged. The sales affected will typically be those where a business is

"The onus is on the buyer to carry out a thorough review of the property and to identify any potential issues"

sold as a 'going concern' or where the sale is of part of a business that can be operated separately.

TOGC can have a beneficial position for us, not only with regards to VAT but also to Stamp Duty Land Tax (SDLT) where significant relief can be achieved. Note that where VAT applies on the purchase price, it will also be charged on SOLT also.

In commercial property transactions a relatively common TOGC acquisition might be to acquire an SPV that has only recently been established for the acquisition of a commercial property which has subsequently secured planning permission or permitted development and the current vendor now wishes to sell to secure a planning gain return.

Stamp Duty Land Tax

For current SDLT rates for commercial property visit the HMRC website at https://www.gov.uk/stamp-duty-land-tax/nonresidential-and-mixed-use-rates.

The table below can be used to calculate the SDLT rate for not only the commercial property purchase but also for a lease premium or a transfer value:

Property, lease premium or transfer value	SDLT Rate
Up to £150,000	Zero
The next £100,000 (£150,001 - £250,000)	2%
The remaining amount (above £250,000)	5%

Example:

Acquiring a freehold commercial property for £465,000, the SDLT liability is calculated as follows:

0% on the first £150,000	= £0	
2% on the next £100,000	= £2,000	
5% on the final £215,000	= £10,750	
Total SDLT	= £12,750	

Legal Entity

Your solicitor will want to understand what legal entity you are buying the property within. Your offer will have been on an assignable basis and have identified which legal entity is making the offer and whether it will be this entity which purchase the property.

In order to establish the legal entity, it is not a complex process. You may choose to do that yourself via a company secretarial service or your accountant. You will need the following:

- Choose a name for your company
- Prepare the Articles of Association
- Prepare the Memorandum of Association
- Decide on VAT registration
- Shareholding agreement
- Bank account

Commercial funding

Commercial funding will take time and needs to be given proper care and attention. It will fundamentally hinge on the terms of the offer and then the valuation and credit approval process. Expect the valuation to be a thorough professional process via the RICS Red Book system as discussed in previous chapters.

The funding application process would look something like this:

- Details of property to possible funders via broker
- Draft term sheets issued by several funders
- Commitment fee paid to selected funder
- KYC/AML of developer and any private investors, sent to broker/funder
- Red Book valuation survey booked
- Funder commences credit paper preparation
- QS report instructed and issued
- Funder submits paper to credit

- Credit backed terms issued
- Credit backed terms accepted
- Commitment fee paid
- Documentation issued for signature
- Independent Legal Advice (ILA) taken and PG's signed
- Insurance evidence provided
- Deal completed and first draw down confirmed

Note that if you have senior debt and also mezzanine, you may have to repeat much of this commercial process in parallel as well as the necessary approvals from senior debt to enable a second charge lender to be engaged. Your commercial broker will support you in navigating this process.

Private Investment

If you have a private investor(s), who are becoming shareholders in your newly formed SPV, you will need to ensure that they are 'on-boarded' in a compliant way, to FCA 13/3 and to the banks approval.

The process will include the following areas of on-boarding:

- Self-Certified Sophisticated Investor Questionnaire
- Investment Memorandum
- Heads of terms
- Loan agreement
- Shareholding/JV agreement
- Reserved matters
- Delegated authorities
- Know Your Client checks
- Anti-Money Laundering (AML) checks
- Company registers
- Transaction cash flow statement
- Banking and mandates

- Data protection
- HMRC
- Articles of Association
- Memorandum of Association
- Board Meeting structure
- Issue of shares
- Understanding roles and responsibilities of your private investor

This can be quite a lengthy and thorough process and should be conducted through your solicitor to make this as smooth as is possible.

Delisting from Business Rates

As you will almost certainly be buying a commercial property, you will be liable for business rates immediately, from the point of purchase. Hence it is vital to control your holding costs that you delist from business rates at the earliest opportunity.

Your primary focus will have been to engage an early works order for a strip out contractor to take possession of the site within days of legal completion and to commence the soft strip out of the property which will, given the correct process, be sufficient to enable the delisting from business rates with the Valuation Office (VOA).

Utilities

At the point of legal completion, you will assume the responsibilities for all utilities. It is your responsibility to mitigate these costs as quickly as possible.

Meter readings must be taken for all utilities – mainly gas, water and electricity and reported to the service provider.

It is important to bear in mind that if you are buying a commercial property, the utility connections are likely to be of a commercial or industrial scale.

Many a developer has been caught out by missing meter readings but another area which you MUST consider is your standing charges for these larger capacity supplies. If you only record and advise of the meter readings you will no longer be responsible for any usage. However, you will almost certainly remain responsible for the standing charges, which for these large commercial/industrial supplies can be many thousands of pounds per annum in their own right – thought provoking indeed!

Ensure that you consult your utility provider and in conjunction with your design team, decide whether you should cap off or disconnect the service entirely.

Pause for thought - Does it make the car go faster?

Those who know me will know that "Does it make the car go faster" is a favourite quote of mine and frequently used. It comes from the accomplished Frank Williams CBE, of Williams F1 motorsport fame who, despite being a tetraplegic after an accident in 1986 resulting in spinal injuries, went on to lead a dynamic business. F1 has been described as a sport for two hours on a Sunday afternoon but a global business for the rest of the year - a great view! Frank Williams knew that his main objective was to win races and hence make his car the fastest and most reliable around the circuit. During his time as a business owner, he was frequently presented with business plans, purchase orders and invoices etc. He became famous for his abrupt analysis and questioning, summarised in one phrase; before approving, he would always ask "Does it make the cargo faster?" Needless to say that if the answer was no, then the purchase order or plan did not get approved!

Clarity and focus on your mission, with every ounce and sinew of resource and energy you have, is critical to the swift and decisive achievement of your objectives and the continuous evolution of your performance and growth. Anything that is non-core to achieving this is automatically relegated to a lower priority, possibly to be revisited another day. So today I ask you: "Do you know what makes YOUR car go faster? and just as importantly, "what does not?!"

10. Business

> *I always like to look on the optimistic side of life, but I am realistic enough to know that life is a complex matter — Walt Disney*

The successful outcome of your development will depend on two primary factors:

1. Operating the development and all the detailed contract management that will be required.

2. Operating an effective business.

We have already established that your commercial conversion or development will be acquired within an SPV. This is a specific legal entity purely for the purposes of supporting your strategy on this development. You are therefore running a business in a company which has a hard asset class of a property within it, rather than running a property development that happens to have the inconvenience of a company to manage!

In selecting the SPV that you will have consciously decided upon, either (typically) a limited company or limited liability partnership, the structure will probably look something like this diagram of an operating Special Purpose Vehicle for a development.

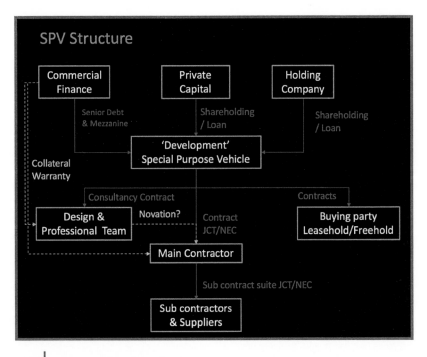

The decisions that you make, at the front end of the development, in deciding which legal entity to house your development in, will affect the tax efficiency and structuring of your development.

It is important to seek good advice from your accountant, tax advisor and solicitor on the right legal entity structure for your particular circumstances and strategy. This is to ensure that you have a robust and clearly effective strategy that works for all the stakeholders that you have in your business.

When establishing any legal entity, we should be mindful that this places serious obligations on us as directors or partners. These obligations should not be underestimated and should be researched thoroughly, with sound advice taken, to ensure that you have the correct training, education and knowledge to carry out your obligations and duties effectively at all times.

These obligations come with fiduciary responsibilities of acting in the best interests of the company and the shareholders at all times. There will be substantial compliance and governance obligations, HMRC & Companies House filings which will be required. You can use your accountant or a company secretarial organisation to operate this effectively and compliantly.

Remember that directorships, as an example, will leave a permanent footprint. Your performance as a director should not be underestimated and your record and your compliance will remain with you at organisations such as Companies House, without being too dramatic, for eternity. Your reputation is the only thing you have so ensure you value and protect this and make rational and well-informed decisions on how you structure organisations and just as importantly, who you structure those with.

With the requirement for your business to raise funding through senior debt development finance, a further set of obligations will be established on you:

- Personal guarantees
- 1st charge on the property
- Debenture on the SPV

So you can see yet again from the above that it is in our interest

"fiduciary responsibilities of acting in the best interests of the company and the shareholders at all times"

as a developer, to house that development in an SPV with only generally a single asset in it. Your senior debt provider will be used to this structure and it also provides clarity that there are no historical trading issues with that organisation such as legacy insurance claims etc. An SPV generally works well for all parties.

Organisational and company structuring is a specialist area and requires significant advice from your professional team. It could also be held within a holding company structure where the shareholding of the SPV, in the case of a limited company, could be held by a holding company as well as by all the organisations and people who may be your joint venture partners, as fellow shareholders.

Typically, this might be a 50%:50% joint venture partner structure or possibly 49%:51%. A joint venture partner could have 50% and your holding company could have 50%. Your accountant and tax advisor will be able to advise you on how best to structure the SPV in context with all your other business operating interests.

This image is an example of how such a structure could operate.

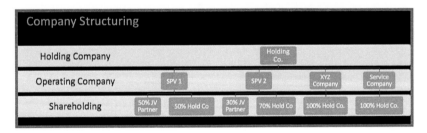

New company checklist

It is helpful to have a checklist to go through a number of key areas which are required to be considered when establishing a new organisation:

1. Name of the organisation - Is this going to be from a

marketing branding perspective or is this going to be a limited company which has no trading value in its name i.e. development 123 Limited.

2. Directors
3. Shareholders
4. Registered address
5. Insurance requirements of the business
6. Delegated authorities required – these are a very clear list of who has what responsibility to what value, when and in what circumstances, so that all directors and shareholders have a clear understanding and accountability structure.
7. Bank account must be set up with a very clear mandate. See separate section on bank accounts.
8. Set of roles and responsibilities of each director
9. Board diary
10. Company secretarial which includes:
    - Articles of Association
    - Memorandum of Association
    - Shareholder agreement
    - HMRC land transaction documents for the new company and the asset there within.

Business bank account

The SPV will require its own bank account. It becomes much more straight forward if you have a bank account per individual company. In some cases, you may choose to have different types of accounts such as client account, savings account and current account for your SPV. Some businesses may utilise one account specifically for tax to ensure that cash flow is separated to aide smooth payments for the business. Having a bank account for business will assist the reconciliation from an accounting perspective and enable the reporting process effectively.

Quite often in developments, joint venture structures exist. It is worth bearing this in mind as you establish your bank account and the obligations that all shareholders will have in their roles and responsibilities. These should be established in the bank mandate to ensure clarity on who has the 'execute and authorise' responsibilities for payment transactions and to what value.

The set up process for bank accounts can vary from 1 to 30 days. If establishing an SPV quickly, such as through a 28 day auction process, consider establishing a bank account in parallel and make the bank account set up a part of your overall master programme.

Bank accounts will almost certainly have daily transaction limits. The location of your shareholders and your ability to use transactions and transfers of significant values for property purchase should be a consideration. Careful planning now will avoid you having to transfer £10,000 - £20,000 per day over multiple days to get a substantial amount transferred.

Location of your local bank may be important if you require large amounts to be transferred across, as one or more directors would have to visit your local bank branch, with your ID, which can be a logistical challenge.

General Data Protection Regulations (GDPR)

The GDPR forms part of the data protection regime in the UK and applied from 25 May 2018.

As developers we handle sensitive personal information ranging from certified ID and proof of address as well as possibly bank account details. It is essential that your development business is GDPR compliant. This is a specialist business subject and compliance is mandatory - failure can result in significant fines.

The GDPR sets out seven key principles:
- Lawfulness, fairness and transparency
- Purpose limitation
- Data minimisation
- Accuracy
- Storage limitation

- Integrity and confidentiality (security)
- Accountability

Much of the sensitive information that may be handled would be through our solicitors. However, a developer would, in all likelihood, be accountable for GDPR compliance and specialist advice should be sought to ensure compliance in your systems.

Targets and Measurements

Any business should always monitor and measure its performance over time. There are many methods to measure and these should be adopted and evolved over time so that they form part of the DNA of your business.

Key Business Indicators (KBI)

Key business indicators will be very specific to your business and not necessarily related to the property development within it. This will be covered under key performance indicators in a later section.

The types of key business indicators which you might consider could be:

- Gross profit
- Pre-funding costs
- Post funding costs
- Earnings before interest and tax
- Return on capital employed
- Return on investment
- Internal rate of return
- Return on time employed
- Cash in the bank versus burn rate
- Overhead cost per month

These are examples and there are many more that you could choose to use for your business.

The compelling drive here is to always understand the economics within your business at all times and how your performance is improving or degrading. If there are challenges ahead, you will gradually acquire the data to anticipate them in advance and have every opportunity - and as long as possible - to put in place remedial action to address the challenges.

Key performance indicators (KPI)

Key performance indicators are a set of performance data which are regularly measured against a consistent benchmark across your particular property asset, in this case through your commercial conversions and developments. They represent a standardised set of metrics which you can utilise and grow a database to measure across all of your developments, in due course over time. These key performance indicators may vary and you may choose to have these separated into commercial conversions and new build developments. Simple examples may include:

- Build cost unit rate (£ sqm)
- Land/property purchase price (£ sqm)
- Professional fees as % of development cost
- Cost of sale as % of GDV
- Sell price (£ sqm)
- Contingency deployment ratio
- Profit forecast v actual
- Private investor ROCE annualised
- Gross development value
- Net profit
- Space utilisation factors
- Capital at risk

These KPIs should be updated regularly through each development and also reversed back into your development appraisal due diligence phase and your development analyser documents, to support latest market-based information. This will help you on your next projects as well as monitoring the current performance of your existing projects.

Insurance

Insurance is a specialist area and will certainly be a requirement to one degree or another, based on:

- Business owner
- Developer
- Strategy obligations
- Senior debt provider

A detailed understanding of your insurance strategy and structure is where an insurance broker will serve your business well as a key part of your professional team.

Some of the levels of insurance that you will need to consider for your business may include:

- Business insurance
- Buildings and contents insurance
- Joint names policy
- Contractors all-risk
- Professional indemnity
- Key man insurance
- Public liability
- Employers liability

There are many variant themes of insurance and your specific strategy must be discussed openly with your insurance broker to ensure you have the correct cover required.

You must always insure the property you are purchasing at the point of exchange. At exchange, you are legally obliged to purchase the building at a period of time in the future (stated in the exchange contract). As mentioned earlier, should that building burn down between the point which you have exchanged and your specific completion date, you will still have to complete on the purchase

- therefore it is vital that full insurance is in place at the point of exchange.

Engagement of your professional team and also your main contractor will be very important in the assurance process of which insurance covers a critical layer of diligence. Your senior debt funder will also be highly observant and will want to understand your insurance structure and the levels of which public liability, professional indemnity and employer's liability cover are engaged. So do bear this in mind, in your due diligence and prequalification of your professional team and main contractor and make the insurance requirements a condition of contract.

Overhead

> *'May I wish you 100 employees' - old Chinese proverb*

This interesting and amusing Chinese proverb is meant as a backhanded parting of ill-will and demonstrates how, in business, we should be careful what we wish for. Building a business with staff and other overheads is not for everyone as it brings a certain type and diversity of skills required to manage people. However, to truly grow a successful business, an overhead is going to be just a matter of time before it is required.

A key decision-making process you will go through undoubtedly during the set up and growth of your company, is how you expand and leverage the business with additional resource and the timing of when you invest in this additional cost – we refer to this as a business overhead.

Think carefully on each decision you make to apply resource to your business and how you engage it. The vision and scale of your business aspirations will have a profound effect on the requirement for an overhead of any size, or not.

Any business will need certain cost centres to function. Traditionally these fit into two categories:

1. Fixed costs – this would include all costs which are not a direct cost of sale and are, therefore, generally fixed irrespective of the level of sale. These might include rent, rates, staff and fees etc. While these costs are frequently necessary to grow your organisation, timing of when you choose to bring these resources on-board, as well as the method of engagement, will be fundamental to your economic efficiency.

2. Variable costs – these will include costs which can be scalable (up and downwards) depending on demand for the service and workload. Often these services are engaged at the formative stages of a business or a project deployment and can be scaled or terminated, at short notice to mitigate any downside, should the need arise. Equally they can be ratcheted up to suit increasing demand and in certain areas could be the intermediate step towards a more permanent investment into a fixed cost.

Many a business has come into harm's way by not spending enough time on managing the efficiencies and timing of overhead costs. A key metric of gross (pre-overhead costs) and net profit (post-overhead costs) will serve you well as you monitor performance towards your business plan's economic growth projections.

The business leader's dilemma will be to ponder the level of overhead required to meet the needs of the business by analysing:

- Current performance and efficiency
- The Business plan
- Projected performance levels
- Changes in market position
- Economic externalities
- Competitor forces
- Market dynamics
- Regular measurement data set
- Funding covenant in place

Too much overhead, too early, will significantly dilute your bottom line and probably more fundamentally, deplete your cash flow to a potentially troubling low level.

Not enough overhead may mean you have created a manageable 'job' for yourself, unable to meet all the demands of a business including sales, marketing, order fulfilment, operations, finance, compliance, governance, health and safety etc and the business performance will suffer and not meet its potential.

One of the significant advantages of being a developer of commercial conversion schemes is that much of the expertise, resource, knowledge and services are there in bountiful supply with up-to-date market experience to serve your needs on a development level engagement, so that you do not have to employ staff and hold a large fixed cost overhead.

It is this great leverage that is a core advantage for us as developers. As you grow your team of professionals to support your business, you will be able to take advantage of the economies of scale of using the same resource increasingly on a repetitive basis. This will not only save you time but also potentially provide significant cost savings as well as growing a mutually beneficial partnership which may lead to unexpected benefits in the future.

A few points to be aware of:

- Past performance of your external partner is by no means a guarantee of future performance.
- Monitor workload levels to ensure capability and resource levels.
- Regularly check covenant strength of partners through prequalification checks.
- Meet regularly with your external partners to check progress, compliance and health of relationship etc.
- Ensure that businesses are aligned in their values, where possible.

Do not be afraid of having an overhead, however do be hugely focused on ensuring it is success-based and controlled with variable costs preferable, rather than high levels of fixed costs. A considered understanding of the phase of business maturity you are in, the market and strategy you are deploying and the funding available, will all play a significant part in establishing your own business policy in this regard.

As developers we have a great opportunity to keep much of our cost base on a development by development basis thus maximising returns and focus while minimising risks at holding company level.

Defining Your Product

The 'product' you are producing is probably the most important decision you will make in the course of your development. It is your core, your very essence. Every decision you make will be purposefully designed to take the product one step closer to fruition.

A 'start with the end in mind' approach will enable you to walk a mile in all stakeholders' shoes at every twist and turn of your future development to help you to create a clear product vision for your business, which could include one or more of the following:

- Studios
- 1 bed apartments
- 2 bed executive/penthouses
- Starter homes
- Affordable homes
- Micro apartments
- Mid-market 3-4 bed houses
- Executive 5 bed houses
- Retail units (in the case of mixed use scheme)

Some of the key questions you will be asking yourself in defining the correct product for your business may be:

- What does society require?
- What will society allow?
- What is fundable?
- What area?
- What are your intentions - hold and rent or sell?

- What is your buying market – young professionals, Help to Buy etc?

It would be safe to say that not all products will be acceptable in all areas. There is limited demand for five bedroom detached executive houses in central London and likewise quite possibly a small market for one bedroom micro-apartments in Norfolk.

I cover this specifically in 'Risk' in the Economics chapter when we take a detailed look at concentration risk.

Designing

For most, the aspiration is not to do just one development. The development is a vehicle to achieve a higher goal or purpose and it is also unlikely that a single development will be sufficient for you to reach your ultimate goal, hence you will probably be undertaking multiple developments.

If you set your sights on the longer term, then quickly you will contextualise the first development as a route to commencing and building your design and specification brief for future developments.

At each stage of your development you are building mini assets which will support the growth of your business and assist in your future developments.

Examples of mini assets around your product may include:

- Design brief
- Specification
- CGIs of typical apartments
- Apartment layouts
- Sales brochures/collateral
- Processes
- Interior design plan
- Interior dressing of apartments

Each development will have its own nuances, however you will be making large incremental steps if you plan for the longer term and view these items as investment as you build your macro interests rather than just a necessary cost for a development.

The quality of fixtures and fittings will be of particular importance as you define your market. Walking a mile in your buyers' shoes will be vital in ensuring you optimise your sales revenue while ensuring a swift route to sale and completion. This will result in paying back expensive development finance (and possibly private investors) in a timely manner to reduce cost of finance and maximising development profitability.

A great design team will enable you to focus your limited budget in the right areas that will satisfy:

- Structural warranties
- Help to Buy
- Your sales agents
- The demand in the market
- Buyer appeal
- Blueprint for your business's continued place in the market.

When a buyer walks into your show apartment they will be looking at visual and practical elements which will catch their eye:

- Natural light
- Quietness
- Aspect
- How light the apartment feels
- Kitchens
- Kitchen work surfaces
- Built-in appliances
- Wine rack
- Heated towel rail
- Fully tiled bathroom
- Where does the TV go?
- Underfloor heating rather than radiators
- They will definitely want high speed broadband mentioned.

Depending on your chosen market and exit, there could well be a different specification for certain elements. For instance, if you were holding and renting you may choose to apply a specification that is more hard wearing and requires less maintenance over the years

Environment sustainability

As developers we have chosen a path of responsibility in being catalytic to the creation of shared value.

The mine and burn fossil fuel economy is simply not sustainable over the long term and this planet only has a finite amount of natural capital. If we are designing and creating buildings that have a design life and leaseholds of in excess of 125 years, we would be remiss not to fully consider environmentally sustainable options thoroughly, particularly as in most cases they make sound economic sense also.

Many of you reading this book will have, or may be considering a family in the future. Therefore long term horizons come into perspective when considering our future generations and the type of world and array of assets that we leave behind for our children as part of our legacy.

The quicker we see this as a business opportunity rather than an imposed burden and not just 'saving the planet', the more integrated our business and personal choices will be over the long term. It is this mindset that is required to truly optimise and transform our vision for the assets we create.

This book focuses on the overall sustainability of your development business however, true sustainability must involve environmental as well as economic sustainability.

"The mine and burn fossil fuel economy is simply not sustainable"

Currently the built environment accounts for approximately:

- 45% of total UK carbon emissions (27% from domestic buildings and 18% from non-domestic).
- 72% of domestic emissions arise from space heating and the provision of hot water.
- 32% of landfill waste comes from the construction and demolition of buildings.
- 13% of products delivered to construction sites are sent directly to landfill without being used.

We must make a decision on whether we want our development business to contribute to the problem or be part of the solution.

"The quicker we see this as a business opportunity rather than an imposed burden and not just saving the planet, the more integrated our business and personal choices will be over the long term"

Without considering the entire life cycle of the building at the start of the design process, we could be missing huge potential for optimising the developments environmental performance. Our main areas of focus will be the 8 stages of the ENTIRE life cycle of a building, namely:

1. Design
2. Transportation
3. Installation
4. Operation
5. Maintenance
6. Refurbishment
7. Demolition
8. Recovery/Recycle

Our aim should be to minimise the effect on the environment by the following:

- CO_2 emission reduction
- Overall reduction in greenhouse gas emissions
- Increase energy efficiency and performance
- Increased renewable energy adoption
- Water reduction
- Waste reduction
- Materials from sustainable sources
- Minimise the use of precious natural capital

What is Natural capital?

Natural capital can be defined as the world's stocks of natural assets which include geology, soil, air, water and all living things.

Why is natural capital an issue?

With financial capital, when we spend too much we run up debt, which if left unchecked, can eventually result in bankruptcy. With natural capital, when we draw down too much stock from our natural environment we also run up a debt which needs to be paid back, for example by replanting clear-cut forests, or allowing aquifers to replenish themselves after we have abstracted water. If we keep drawing down stocks of natural capital without allowing or encouraging nature to recover, we run the risk of local, regional or even global ecosystem collapse.

Poorly managed natural capital therefore becomes not only an ecological liability, but a social and economic liability too. Working against nature by overexploiting natural capital can be catastrophic, not just in

"We must make a decision on whether we want our development business to contribute to the problem or be part of the solution"

"we can challenge tradition making it possible for a building to become a net EXPORTER of power in the future"

terms of biodiversity loss, but also catastrophic for humans as ecosystem productivity and resilience decline over time and some regions become more prone to extreme events such as floods and droughts. Ultimately, this makes it more difficult for human communities to sustain themselves, particularly in already stressed ecosystems, potentially leading to starvation, conflict over resource scarcity and displacement of populations.

Source: World Forum on Natural Capital

https://naturalcapitalforum.com

This is another area where modular construction, undertaken correctly has the opportunity to create massive sustainability advantages and we will look at this in more detail in a future chapter.

Other emerging areas of technological advancement which will aide environmental performance will include:

- The Internet of Things (IoT) & Integrated Automated Building Systems
- Greywater Plumbing Systems
- Electrochromic Glass
- Solar Thermal Cladding
- 3D printing
- Self-healing concrete
- High quality maintenance

Energy remains one of the largest and most impactful industries we have and one which is undergoing a transformation to address years of neglect in environmental terms. Energy also represents one of our largest cost base from a building owners perspective.

To turn this conundrum on its head, we can challenge tradition making it possible for a building to become a net EXPORTER of power in the future.

By focusing on two key areas we can get closer to this point whilst still achieving economic sustainability in parallel and that is the point here – you can have your cake and eat it. These two areas are:

- Driving energy consumption down
- Increasing energy production

Decentralised energy represents an economic solution to an ageing and creaking centralised energy system which has inherent inefficiencies and losses in its distribution system, all of which come at a cost to the environment and the economic equation. Additionally, given that heat is a by-product of energy production, efficient generation of energy close to its point of use enables us to utilise the heat generated and commodotise it as a valuable product in its own right, rather than a waste product. We have been involved in:

- enabling many decentralised energy developments including district heating systems.
- enabling incredible levels of community shared value through logical thinking.

Many solutions exist that will enable minimum, if any, trade-off for challenging tradition and taking your development down a route of high performance environmentally sustainable credentials. Indeed this could be the differentiator for you in tomorrow's market that makes your property unique, stands out and a more intelligent investment with dramatically lower operational costs, more secure and possibly with additional income streams.

Types of renewable energy which are being adopted and form part of your designers checklist include:

- Ground source heat pumps
- Air source heat pumps
- Solar thermal
- Solar photovoltaic

- Biomass
- Wind
- Energy storage
- Intelligent control systems

Each of these technologies should be carefully selected and adopted on solid investment principles such as funding ROI and IRR calculations.

There are of course many more variant themes of renewable energy and energy reduction methods which your designer will review and discuss with you.

Let me pose a question from a Freeholders perspective: 'walk a mile in another

"This is an opportunity to provide socially conscious businesses with products that align with their environmental policies, bottom line positioning and long term shareholder returns"

person's shoes'. Would you pay more for the freehold interests of the property if the building not only had a very low energy consumption, was operationally intelligent and had an effective and minimal maintenance cost base, but also had an additional income stream of energy exporting back to the grid?

This may provide the freeholder a great marketing opportunity to command high rental premiums whilst also providing additional energy security on site. Most publically traded organisations have a mandate committed to their sharehlders to operate environmentally effectively and every area of business activity is and will become scrutinised, including that of leases and the type of properties that are occupied. This is an opportunity to provide socially conscious businesses with products that align with their environmental policies, bottom line positioning and long term shareholder returns.

This would be much more appealing especially given the challenges that the leasehold/freehold market structuring is facing at present.

The forward thinking funders are beginning to take an increased interest in this area and in the future I expect environmental

"organisations like the European Investment Bank (EIB) and United Nations (UN) adopting this approach"

sustainability to sit within the evaluation and due diligence criteria of funders and investors.

There are many interesting initiatives and processes that are emerging that are lead indicators as to where the world or business may be going, including:

- Carbon cost accounting
- Natural capital accounting
- Green bonds
- Social impact bonds – remember our section earlier on how society is moving from an input based to an output based economy?

Environmental, Social and Governance (ESG) is a set of standards and criteria that increasingly socially conscious investors use for due diligence and screening of their investments.

It considers how a company/investment opportunity stands scrutiny in each of the 3 areas.

Environmental criteria considers the stewardship of the natural environment. Social criteria scrutinises how it manages relationships with customers, employees, suppliers and the communities where it operates.

Governance observes how the company operates from shareholder structure and rights, leadership, internal controls and audit.

When you have organisation's like the European Investment Bank (EIB) and United Nations (UN) adopting this approach there will inevitably be much attention from the funding markets and sovereign wealth funds which will filter down to partial adoption and beyond, in the years to come.

The UN Principles of responsible investing are:

- We will incorporate environmental, social and corporate governance (ESG) issues into investment analysis and decision-making processes.

- We will be active owners and incorporate ESG issues into our ownership policies and practices.
- We will seek appropriate disclosure on ESG issues by the entities in which we invest.
- We will promote acceptance and implementation of the principles within the investment industry.
- We will work together to enhance our effectiveness in implementing the principles.
- We will each report on our activities and progress towards implementing the principles.

Examples of ESG criteria used by investors include determining a company's impact on climate change or carbon emissions, water use or conservation efforts, anti-corruption policies, board diversity, human rights efforts and community development.

Much work remains to be done in this area. However, I hope this has given you food for thought and the context, opportunity, accountability and responsibility that we as developers automatically assume when we take on our deeply meaningful societal role. Whether and to what extent we choose to adopt environmental sustainability could well have a fundamental effect on our economic sustainability in the future and the valuation on our business.

"to what extent we choose to adopt environmental sustainability could well have a fundamental effect on our economic sustainability in the future and the valuation on our business."

Marketing

The dilemma for any developer in selling their units is that a higher sales value will generally result from a finished apartment being able to be viewed.

This, however, does leave sales towards the back end of the development when you ideally would be wanting to have significant sales converted to pay back the development finance as quickly as possible.

Hence your strategy could be formed in four key steps:

1. Very Early: Sold pre-development – quite frequently this may be in a block to an institutional investor on a non-title split basis.

2. Early: Off plan with computer generated graphics (CGIs) – this will generally be during the early construction phase of the development where only external access may be possible (if at all) for potential viewers. Many people struggle to visualise what a building site could become, or may not be able to visit the development, hence enabling them to visualise the finished product is vital.

3. Middle: Show apartment – this will be in the middle stages of a development and will be a great opportunity to stage the property in the very best light with full dressing of furniture and decoration. It should be like walking into the home of your dreams.

4. Late: Actual, not a 'typical' dressed apartment - this would be a similar approach to 3 (above) where the actual apartment to buy is fully dressed rather than a sample apartment. Frequently this would be used to push the last few sales of apartments to conclude the development.

If you are designing and constructing a show apartment, make sure that you programme your accelerated works with your main contractor carefully to ensure you do not incur variation costs for 'out of sequence works'. The works should be properly sequenced to ensure your sales agent has a plan to work towards and your main contractor understands this key deliverable.

On a sell exit strategy, you will be selling the freehold interests of the property as well. This would mean that a 12 apartment conversion (in England and Wales) would have:

- 12 leasehold sales
- 1 freehold sale

Showcasing

All of the hard work that you have put into the finding, funding, designing and constructing your new apartments will all culminate in your ability to sell them. The very best team to present your product to the market in a well-structured and sequenced manner will pay you a great return on investment. Your primary ways of doing this will include:

- Brochure and sales collateral
- Sales agent

- Internal resource
- Imagery - on site hoarding
- Website
- Social Media
- Computer generated images – CGIs
- Augmented Reality and Virtual Reality
- Dressed show apartments

This is a specialist area which is also facing stiff competition in the market as the world of estate agency undergoes significant pressure to its traditional model. However, having said that, when you are selling a large number of units that are supporting expensive development finance, think long and hard about trying to 'nickel and dime' the back end sales. The financial viability of your business may depend on it!

It is my experience that if buyers can make the bridge between visualising the end product and actual seeing it – touching, feeling and walking around it – then they will potentially pay a premium and trigger the sale much quicker.

To showcase your apartments in the best light, your interior designer will establish a colour palette that suits the development, the market mood and fashion of the time. They will also design the furniture and dressings required to enable a shell apartment to be converted into a walk-in home of the buyer's dreams.

A decision you will have to make is whether you offer a choice of specification to your buyer. This might include:

- Kitchen cupboards
- Work surfaces
- Floor finishes
- Wall paint colours
- Tile designs
- Appliances

If you offer this service, it will provide a very personal bespoke approach which will appeal to many clients. However, be wary of the implications on the logistics of managing such a process, the build programme and the order and timeliness of your sales.

The Pros:
- A bespoke home and feel
- Designed for 'You'
- Additional income stream for premium service
- Additional extra packages
- Attracts early buyers

The Cons:
- Additional burden of time
- Relationship and contract with main contractor
- Logistics and administration
- Timing of sales not matching timing of construction
- Complications
- What if a sale fails late in process?

This is a specialist market and if you were to consider it, then possibly you may choose to only allow this for a certain proportion of the units to drive additional early sales before a cut-off timeline in the programme.

Pause for thought - Your Largest Investor.....

"The largest investor you never had is the one that you never knew was watching you" - Mark Stokes

Countless times I have had someone drop me a line asking if we could arrange a coffee and once we got to know each other better, the conversation turned towards that of them wishing to be an investor (sophisticated!).

The point here is that you simply never know who is watching and listening to you and how you behave.

I hear and see a lot of things on social media - ranting, raving, and swearing etc, all of which seeks to build a perceived profile of you, your beliefs and your values in the eyes of the listener. Obviously none of us are 'all things to all people' and the beauty of humanity is to have the freedom to be yourself and not who someone else says you should be.

Our investors and I suspect yours too, are looking for passion and commitment and are also probably aware that things do not always go to plan. They are looking for great communicators who are open, transparent and build confidence through an unshakeable and unflappable drive to use logic, tenacity and calmness to get the best out of teams and deliver as close to certain outcomes that is possible.

What some will tire of very quickly is irrational, volatile and emotional outbursts which, frankly add little to the situation and cause more consternation and concern rather than clarity, courage of conviction and gritty steely determination to do what it takes to secure the most favourable and compliant outcomes possible.

11. Construction

We cannot solve our problems with the same thinking we used when we created them
- Albert Einstein

FINDING

DUE DILIGENCE

PLANNING

VALUATION

EXIT

YOU

STRATEGY

FUNDING

CONSTRUCTION

BUSINESS

COMPLETION

ECONOMICS

The construction phase of a project can be a daunting part of any development. To the unwary, it is filled with mystery, risk and uncertainty. Moving into a different sector, in this case the construction sector, requires a different level of expertise.

With a simple set of systems and the right professional team on board, many of these challenges can be overcome to enable the construction phase to be one of the most rewarding and enlightening parts of any development and to enthuse you with confidence to continue this great strategy with increasing knowledge, awareness and inner confidence.

This is where your development moves from the drawing board and into real-life where you can physically see, in a gratifying way, the project develop, come to life and actually create the physical units you have carefully been nurturing and planning for the previous weeks, months and in some cases, years.

It is true to say the construction phase of any conversion and development project is probably the riskiest stage. I don't think there are many that would disagree with this statement and in particular the funders share that view. They understand that only upon opening up the ground, demolishing the building and stripping out the existing fabric, do you finally understand every nook and cranny of the building or property.

These risks are all identifiable and I would encourage you to understand that there is no risk that has not been encountered by anybody previously. Therefore, having the right professional team on board, understanding what risk is, analysing the risk associated with your particular development and taking the time and having the tenacity to look at and anticipate the solutions required to approach each and every risk and to maximise the opportunity that exists in your building, will ensure that your project has a very high chance of success.

In the construction phase we are focusing on the engagement, under contract, of a main contractor who will undertake all of the refurbishment and construction activities required to create your final product, be that of new-build homes, commercial units or apartments.

The construction phase can generally be split into two particular areas:

1. Pre-contract - leading up to the signing and engagement of your main contractor.
2. Post-contract - the activities following the signing of the contract and the deployment of the obligations therein.

The timing in your overall development timeline on when you undertake your pre-contract activities will be highly dependent on the financial structure of your individual development.

Generally, your funder and indeed yourselves as the primary stakeholder in your development, will require as much certainty as possible of the contractor's obligations, their deliverables and their price for undertaking the work to make sure that the construction cost is very clear in your development economics.

This will have a bearing of the amount of financial leverage you can secure in funding your development. However, all developers have different circumstances. You may already own a land/building or you may be funding it in different ways so we cannot be too generic in this area. However, let us assume for these purposes that the pre-contract and post-contract element is something that we are prepared to invest in our professional team to operate throughout the period between exchange and legal completion of your development.

This will enable us to have all the requisite documentation ready to be signed at the point when you are legally able to complete on the purchase. Therefore, enabling your construction phase of the project to commence immediately after legal completion of the purchase of the property has happened. From an efficiency point of view, this means that your expensive funding solution is set to work immediately and time is of the essence.

As mentioned previously though you must ensure that your main contractor appointment is based on the most accurate and detailed information and requirements as is possible, as changes later down the line become very expensive in terms of cost and time.

The Pre-Contract Phase

The pre-contract phase consists of all the activities required to identify exactly what you, as a developer, require as the finished product for your development and all the sub-activities required in order for you to effectively engage a main contractor to undertake the construction activities. When employing a main contractor, it is important that you engage as much certainty in the process as possible as this process is trying to establish, without any doubt, the absolute requirements and who bears the responsibility of those requirements, for delivering your end product.

The key areas in any contract are as follows:

1. Product or service requirements under the contract.
2. Programme period for the construction.
3. The Cost
4. Dependencies - information/access etc.
5. How - the conditions you want the contract to operate under.
6. Pricing and the mechanism for payment that you will be contracting under.
7. The legally binding roles and obligations of each party under the contractor.

What are likely to be the key elements of your pre-contract phase?

1. Planning of the activities. Pre-contract will be a fairly complex phase which will involve one or more members of your professional team. It is important that everybody is clear on working to a timetable of all events required to achieve your objectives of appointment of your main contractor.
2. Make sure that you have a clear design and all statutory obligations therein, that you wish your builder to comply with. Any uncertainty in this design portion, however it is constructed, could have serious ramifications on your main

contract as changes made on paper are relatively inexpensive. By contrast, changes made in full flight construction can be seriously expensive and create additional cost and time through variations, through additional monies expended and additional time which is also additional cost expended.

3. The due diligence on your main contractors who are tendering

4. Checking, verifying all the detail of course visibility and surveys.

5. Your procurement methodology and contract type. Be very clear on the type of contract you are contracting on, both to your design team and your main contractor. This will convey the requirements for quality, time and cost for your project. You will consider how you identify the balance of detail of your requirements while giving your main contractor the ability to bring their expertise to bear and use the right methodology for them to give you the product in the most efficient manner.

6. The tendering process and how you will manage the risk.

A final point to highlight in gaining as much certainty as time will allow in the design and tendering period, is to assess the impact of variations which will have an exponential impact on your development economics. Any changes during construction could well incur additional costs and time. If a particular task is on the master programme critical path then you will have the added cost of additional bank interest as the development duration will be extended, causing potentially serious ramifications for you, the lender and the private investors.

Procurement

The method of procurement that you deploy can be quite complex and it is something you should consider with your professional team. The areas that you focus on may include:

Design responsibility

1. Cost certainty

2. Programme certainty

3. Quality and predictability of the end product

4. Early stage engagements of your contractor.

There can be many different procurement methods, but the three which are more frequently employed are:

1. Traditional contracting - This will enable great control on quality, the responsibility on the client for design changes and enable the contractor to focus on their core elements of activities in contracting the end product.

2. Design and build - This will have far less detail and therefore, a greater responsibility on the main contractor to use their experience in design to create the end product whilst conforming with the performance specification. Arguably, this can enable a greater control on cost for us as a developer and can be quicker, although control of the end product needs to have a huge amount of focus as does the interpretation of the performance specification and how it is applied to the specific development.

3. Contractors design portions (CDP) - This may enable the best of both worlds, where you have:

> a. Detailed specification in a traditional manner for certain aspects of the design that may be fundamental to your product or that you have evaluated need to be de-risked with up front design.

> b. CDP on certain elements, which may include ground works or the mechanical and electrical building services elements, etc where the contractor has the responsibility to work towards the end product using their skill and design expertise under the performance specification.

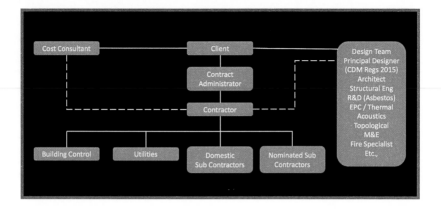

A typical structure of how your contract management will be operated is included in this image.

There are many forms of contract that you can utilise depending on your method of contracting with your main contractor. Some standard model forms of contract include:

- JCT – Joint Contracts Tribunal
- RIBA – Royal Institute of British Architects
- NEC - New Engineering Contract

There are others but these are generally the ones frequently employed. It is also worth considering at the very early stages the method and type of contract you will engage your professional team.

We could use the RIBA or the ACE agreement for this engagement at an early stage.

These are the generally accepted model forms of contract which will take you through, step by step, all of the pre-requisite requirements of the contract and enable you and your professional team to draft a suite of contracts for your development that will be readily accepted by:

- Main contractor
- Professional team
- Funders

- Developer

There will of course be negotiation along the way, however this will generally be around the specific clauses of contract.

Funder requirements

The pre-contract phase is an important part of engaging the main contractor and one equally important part of your team you should not ignore in this process is your senior debt funder. They may wish to approve, in principle, which main contractor you are intending to use. Please make sure that you build this into your contracting timeline. Without this, you will not be able to draw down funding from your senior debt provider.

Why would your senior debt provider be interested in which contractor you choose? Well, let us look at what they are lending on. Your senior debt provider will generally be lending a percentage of loan-to-cost on the purchase of the development, but also on the development finance. In doing this, they need to assure themselves that the correct expertise is in place through the main contractor and the correct assurance methodology.

They will want to ensure the main contractor is competent to undertake the work, and that they have a strong and robust covenant. Should the developer go out of business, for whatever reason, the funder will ensure they have a contractual 'look through' to the main contractor. This is called a collateral warranty and is a pre-established contract that becomes engaging under certain default events, such as the developer becoming insolvent for instance.

If the developer should fail for whatever reason, the main contractor has the obligation, under contract, with the senior funder (through the collateral warranty) who still has funds at hand, to deploy the remainder of the work as they only pay based on monthly applications certified in arrears, based on work undertaken. This ensures the development has every chance of success in arriving at the end product, in a worst case scenario, with or without the developer!

Your funder must be engaged at the early stages and it will give them a lot of assurance to know that you have a strong professional team on board and that you have a clear timetable, getting to the main contractor selection. Also that you have the requisite form of contract and the clauses within that contract that satisfy the funder.

So what might the funder require? In summary, areas you will need to consider at pre-contract stage for your funders due diligence and verification include:

- Main contractor covenant
- Main contractor suitability
- Designer warranty
- Model form of contract
- Collateral warranty provision
- Insurance
- Structural warranty provider

Selecting your professional team

At the pre-contract phase, it's important to ensure you've engaged the correct professional team. Your team should be selected through thorough research based on the factors covered in previous chapters. Arrange and structure meetings where you can meet the actual individuals within your intended professional team, to ensure you can form a strong relationship with them.

Once selected, make sure you get named individuals in the contract – think about it – have you ever been promised the A Team and ended up with the B Team!

Consult with planners, contractors, other developers and with your general network and ask for recommendations of successful projects and the professional team that was deployed on them.

Taking up references is extremely important. Once you have a shortlist of your professional team, ensure they are accredited to their various bodies and have a quality control registration. Check their professional insurance levels, their previous experiences, past projects, type of construction and type of location they have worked in.

Check which forms of contract they are happy to contract on. Issue an outline scoping document stating your requirements and request for a detailed proposal. Upon receipt of the proposal, review each element and finally, interview the shortlist of your professional team before making your final appointments and placing them under contract.

The RIBA have a list of eight sections of work phases that any development will pass through. These are areas that you can cross-check against the level of detail and duration of each appointment you make with your professional team:

1. Strategic definition of the development
2. Preparation and brief
3. Concept design
4. Developed design
5. Technical design
6. Construction phase
7. Handovers and closeouts
8. End use phase

When selecting your main contractor, use your professional team and in particular, your quantity surveyor. They will know the market place, the main contractors typically interested in your scope of work and they will have existing relationships and experiences on previous projects.

Doing your due diligence is absolutely essential – we know it needs to be bank grade!

It is recommended that there are a number of phases for your due diligence in selecting your contractor:

1. Draw up a long list of main contractors. This might be between 8-10 contractors who are known in the local area and who have done previous projects and other developments that you or your professional team have had experience of.

2. Do credit checks properly on each of the contractors. This is important to understand whether they have the correct level of covenant that your senior debt funder would be happy with.

3. Take reference checks on each one of the developers.

4. Send a pre-qualification questionnaire out to each of the developers asking for their detailed response. This can be an exhaustive list of questions covering compliance and the structure and positioning of the company. Make sure they have the correct covenant, capacity, financial strength, individual skills required and the resources to carry out your development.

Once you've taken up references, you will then reduce your pre-qualified list down to a short list and you will be able to compare the credentials of your short list contractors - if this is your final list, you release the tendering information too.

When releasing final invitation to tender documents to each party on that short list, generally this would be somewhere in the region of 4-5 tendering parties. If you tender to more parties than that, then contractors may not take you seriously, because their chances strongly diminish of securing the work.

Tendering of any project is an expensive exercise and failure to secure tendered work for a main contractor means it is an abortive cost to the business. So treat your contractor's resources with respect and ensure that you do not go out to too many parties. Therefore, have a very clear opportunity for your contractor to secure the work. If you tender to three contractors as an example, then one contractor may have a large contract award and decline to tender, another may drop out through other reasons, part way through the contracting period.

Our end objective is to have a minimum of three fully compliant tender returns. We must try and avoid a situation where we only have 2 tenders: we have one bid that is high, one bid that is low and we don't know which one is right. If we have three bids, the likelihood is we will have two close together and

"Our end objective is to have a minimum of three fully compliant tender returns"

one possibly adrift, giving us a better idea about compliance and a true market rate.

The invitation to tender structure which the contractors will receive, may include sections such as:

- Contract preliminaries,
- Architectural specification,
- Architectural and structural schedule of works,
- Electrical services specification,
- Mechanical services specification,
- Final summary form of tender Appendices,

Following the release of invitations to tender (ITT) to your main contractors, your professional team will hold mid-tender interviews, which will enable any tender queries to be answered and for you and your professional team to understand the level of interest the contractors are showing in the project and how their team are approaching the contract.

There will also be a clear 'request for information' process where any tender queries can be received and issued as notes of clarification to the tendering parties. The more questions you answer and the clearer you make the requirements, the less risk that the main contractor will include on their tender submission and also the fewer qualifications they will make to their submission too.

The tender documentation will prescribe a very clear time and date of when tenders are to be returned.

Your professional team should open, independently verify and report the opening of these tenders and their high level content, at a particular time and record the initial key data as part of your governance process.

How will you know what information to record at tender opening stage? Well the professional team will agree a tender return compliance form which will have all relevant data and approvals relating to the bid. You can request that you attend the opening should you wish, as the client.

The following days and in some cases weeks, will be taken up with the examination of those tenders and drawing up a like-for-like comparison. There may well then be a tender negotiation where each one of the tenderers is asked to clarify certain parts of their bid, asked to look at revisiting certain elements and answering any particular queries. Then you will have a very clear understanding of what each bid contains.

The initial tender opening ceremony, recorded lowest bid may not end up being the lowest bid at the end of the adjudication process. Remember you are looking for the most compliant, most efficient bid at final account stage at completion of the contract. Do not be tempted to take the initial lowest bid, as there may well be issues which will surface throughout the course of the contract.

It is the final account certainty that you are looking for. So ask the tough questions in the good times at tender stage and ensure that you get the right price. Do not be fooled by taking the low price and assuming other additional cost will not follow.

It can be common practice to have a final part of the process, which is known as 'best and final offer' (or BAFO), where you go back out to some, or all of the tenderers for their final bid which encompasses all the final post tender queries. Then the final decision making is required to appoint the contractor, under the terms of the contract that has been negotiated.

Once the contract has been negotiated, allow sufficient time for the preparation of the contract documents and all the contract particulars. This will generally be done by your professional team.

There should be a pre-start meeting with your main contractor where your professional team and your main contractor meet and look at all the requirements of the project, how the initial phase of the project will be executed, how communication will be maintained throughout the course of the project, reports and meetings and how obligations and responsibilities will be rolled out. You will probably evolve a standard meeting agenda for this meeting.

Create a schedule of all your progress meetings and valuations and make sure the stipulations from your funder are known, clear to your main contractor and everyone is aware of the diarised dates – this will be key to the cash-flow of the development for all parties.

Make sure all statutory obligations are also met. Also discuss with your main contractor how they will take possession of the site, what the dependencies are and when.

The main contractor will have indicated within their tender return, the mobilisation time they require to commence the contract. If there are delays in you being able to contract and hand the site possession to them for whatever reason, keep open communication with the main contractor. They will have other contracts which they are securing, which will be competing for their valuable resources such as project management team, so be open and frequent so that they understand and can manage any initial delays on award of contract. We recently had a situation where the main contractor held their team available for 3 months whilst a legal issue delayed the legal completion and hence, our ability to award the contract.

As well as ensuring the availability of the management team is reserved, the cost of building materials and labour may increase if delays are rather more significant. There can only be a certain defined period of time between when the main contractor tender, often referred to as 'tender validity period', expires and will need to be revalidated. This is generally between 4-12 weeks and is something you can stipulate in the tender documents as a compliance point.

When your contractor takes possession of the site they will probably become responsible for the utility costs on site, hence a new set of meter readings should be taken to ensure the main contractor is responsible for any further gas, water and electricity consumption from this point onwards.

Ask your professional team to undertake a full condition survey of the property and the surrounding area so that any damage caused to roads, curbs and fences etc can be pre-identified, leaving any issues that happen on site to be easily traced to the main contractor's possession period. The condition survey would usually consist of photographs, video and an accompanying written report signed off by the professional team and the main contractor for agreement of accuracy.

The contract documents will then be prepared and signed with the main contractor. This can be done initially through a Letter Of Intent (LOI). However, ideally, with the correct planning you will be entering into the main form of contract signed with your main contractor once all items have been negotiated. This will include a clear start and possession date.

Within the contract, the main contractor's responsibilities for Health and Safety, particularly under the CDM regulations, will be very clear. This is an important part of the process and Construction, Design and Management regulations are a key responsibility of the various parties under the contract.

The three main parties in the UK under the CDM regulations will be the client, which will be you as the developer, principal designer and principal contractor. The principal designer will take full responsibility of all of the design process. This may be part of your consideration when selecting your professional team to appoint your principal designer and all obligations sit within that designer, such as Health and Safety or any of the other project requirements. This can aid the communication throughout the entire project.

Likewise, this is a similar process for your principal contractor where you are appointing one party and allowing them to use their expertise to deploy, through sub-contractors and suppliers, their obligations. As a client, it is your responsibility to notify the HSE through an F10 notice that the project is underway and also employing the Principal Contractor and the Principal Designer.

Cost Management

The success or failure of your development in realising healthy returns for the shareholders and stakeholders will primarily depend on maintaining a solid and resolute focus on your costs. Your costs will fundamentally affect the profitability of your scheme and should be monitored closely, not just by yourself, but will also be monitored by the monitoring surveyor from your senior debt funder on a monthly basis. They may also come under some degree of scrutiny by your private investors, depending on your method of engagement.

Here are 4 fundamentals of cost management which should be scrutinised throughout any development:

1. Know your costs - This should be in every element, whether it be costs through initial seed capital, professional team, utilities, construction or the sales process. Every single cost should be managed.

2. Control of your costs - Each cost should have an approval against them and should be monitored to ensure there are no variations, or that variations are managed appropriately and authorised to avoid any disputes or nasty surprises later down the line.

3. Monitor your costs - Your cost will change – hopefully they will not, however let us be realistic – we cannot anticipate every foreseeable eventuality. Variations will be almost certain in any project due to any unforeseen events or changes of circumstances. However, you can manage and monitor the impact of these through monitoring variations and also building in:

- Contingency sums
- Provisional sums – a sum for labour and materials for an undetermined scope of work such as removing asbestos or underground obstructions in ground work
- Prime cost sums – a sum identified for a specific item of work such as kitchens or tiles

  These will help, in part, to ensure that this potential does not affect the underlying economics of your development.

4. Take prompt action - This is often missed, with some developers choosing to bury their head and assuming cost escalation will correct itself at the end of the day. It never does! Always take prompt, pro-active measures at the early stage to ensure all information you provide is of the highest quality and as detailed as is required, to ensure everybody has a clear understanding.

The costs that are provided against the specification will form part of your budget for the development, so manage that budget

"Contingency management is crucial"

diligently and monitor the costs to date and the anticipated cost to complete, on a daily/weekly basis through to the end of the contract. It will be your lifeline, it will enable you and all parties to have clarity and all arrive at the finishing line with a sweet taste of success and the economics preserved in the contract.

Contingency management is crucial. Contingency is hallowed and is there in the case of any unforeseen events arriving. These four cost management fundamentals will save you a lot of heartache along the way.

We have mentioned in an earlier chapter the importance of having a very detailed, but highly agile, development analyser. The development analyser, I would suggest to you, would only really be appropriate up to the point of having the offer accepted and approaching exchange of contracts.

What management tools are required to manage the rest of the development, which is still 95% of the time left? Two key trackers are required amongst a host of systems and processes:

- Contract management
- Cash flow management

Contract Management tracking

The contract management tracker is crucial in understanding the cost of management, structuring and controlling of all contracts that are entered into. These contracts may include your main contractor build or refurbishment contracts. It could be any specialist trades that are required ancillary to that main contract, or utility costs, gas, water, electric, mains water, drainage, all aspects of the professional team and any engagements with agents at whatever stage of the contract. This could be retained commercial agents at the front-end or estate agents selling your apartment or housing units at the back-end of your development.

Each and every one of these contracts will generally have a fixed price lump sum, but may be subject to variations under certain circumstances. It is fundamental that you track your contracted value, costs to date and anticipated cost to complete, including any variations under the contract.

Bear in mind that variations can be positive or negative. It may have been decided to include prime cost and provisional sums in contracts that cover areas, which may in the end, not come to fruition and therefore, variations can reduce the contract sum, as well as increase it.

The culture of openness and transparency will provide a helpful backbone to your relationships with all contracted parties. It will help ensure the obligation and duty of care is supported with a constant stream of communication from your professional team and contractors on any indication that variations may occur. This would include a notice from your contractor, informing that they believe there could be an early warning sign of a variation. This will enable you to investigate at the earliest stage and work with your contractor and professional team to mitigate any potential cause and effect, should that variation materialise.

Your senior debt provider's monitoring surveyor will also take comfort and utilise your development tracker to a certain extent. They will want to understand to what extent the project is on track and therefore, within its economic viability parameters. The relevant parts of the contract management tracker can be shared with the monitoring surveyor on the basis of transparency.

The development portion of the senior debt lenders facility will almost certainly be drawn down on a 'monthly in arrears basis'. This will be drawn down against a very clear set of allowable costs, primarily from your professional team and your main contractor.

On a monthly basis, your main contractor will provide you with an application for payment which will be checked by the monitoring surveyor via a site visit. Check that your main contractor is applying for the correct sums of work done, to the pre-agreed contract terms. Once they are happy and have certified the sum with developer and contractor, funds will be transferred usually within 2-10 days.

It is incredibly important during the contract negotiation and agreement phase, with your main contractor, to ensure that the flow of funds to your main contractor from the bank via yourselves allows for sufficient time to ensure that the development is always in the cash flow positive position. The Construction Act that governs construction industry payments does not allow 'paid when paid' clauses, hence it is vital to properly manage the timing of payments in, out and pending from your senior debt provider and transfers to your main contractor.

Cash flow management

Your second primary tool throughout the management of your development will be your cash flow management tool. This will be a fundamental pillar in managing your development as a business and in fact should be a priority for ANY business.

"Cash flow, cash flow, cash flow!"

Your development will be operated in a special purpose vehicle and should have its own bank account as previously discussed in detail. The cash flow management tracker will take the development tracker information and the previous development analyser information and turn it into a month-by-month cash flow management tool.

This will look at the starting bank balance within the company. It will look at all the income and outgoings on a monthly basis and will look at the balance at the end of the month. In some cases, a month-by-month reconciliation will not be enough and you may choose or be required to do this on a week-by-week basis.

All cash inflow must be monitored. This could include:

- Private investor deposits
- Private investor advances
- Own working capital as a private investor to the company
- Senior loan advance for the land purchased
- Mezzanine funding advanced
- Development funding drawdown

All costs, line by line, must be included and scheduled. Only when this detailed information is provided will you be able to understand where the starting and finishing bank balance at the end of each week, or the end of each month, will be.

When understanding how much additional private capital is required for your development, over and above the senior debt and possibly mezzanine, you must derive the private capital requirement from a working cash flow management model. In EquaGroup our detailed model very quickly ensures that we understand the maximum working capital required to be injected into the business to ensure the bank balance not only remains in the positive, but also ensures that a surplus cash flow is retained in the organisation's bank account for unforeseen situations.

Let us think through this scenario where a main contractor applies for a variation, which is bona fide and approved by you, however either the variation is not supported by the senior debt provider or possibly insufficient contingency remains. In this case, a further injection of capital may be required. This would clearly be a drastic situation but can happen so ensure the clear sensitivities of cash flow management are controlled.

Another critical area, which is important to your cash flow, will be the impact of VAT - who charges you VAT, how you claim your VAT back from HMRC, how long does it take to become VAT registered and how that can affect the cashflow.

Programming and planning

Your development will require a high-level strategic programme. This is important for many reasons. It's important for you as a developer to understand exactly where you are in driving the timelines to meet your objectives and also holding to account all parties under contract, to support the achievement of those objectives.

"It is good practice to have a drop-down line on your programme which shows actual versus forecast performance"

Your plan must not be confused with planning and is your overall master programme which should include a

Gantt Chart which ideally should include logic-linked task bars.

The main contractor should be fully aware of this type of programme and this should be identified as part of the tendering process to ensure that once in contract, you have a very clear development programme for which the main contractor has added a significant proportion of the detail to it.

This detailed programme will identify all the key milestones, all the interdependencies within the programme and will illustrate the float in the programme. As an example, a delay in one activity may not necessarily delay the actual end date. Your contractor must ensure that their programme is updated on a regular basis and bring to your attention any potential changes and the extension of time.

The advantage of logic linked detailed programmes is that a critical path sequence of events materialises. This is very helpful when analysing variations in particular and where delays may occur. Any task that lies on the critical path sequence, if extended, through a delay, would impact the completion date. The critical path is fluid and will change as you extend certain tasks and shorten others, hence regular monitoring of all lines within the programme is important.

Should acceleration be required in the programme to hit an important deadline such as practical completion, it is helpful to understand which items if directly accelerated would bring about the quickest outcome. As some tasks are not on the critical path, incurring additional costs in accelerating them with no impact on the completion date may not be a wise use of funds.

It is good practice to have a drop-down line on your programme which shows actual versus forecast performance. This will assist the monitoring of progress and any early warning signs of slippage in the programme which can be discussed, root cause identified and any corrective action taken to remedy.

Progress reporting

The main contractor and your professional team must provide you regular formalised progress reporting updates, which will be a requirement in their contract.

Included in the main contractor's monthly report should be:

- Health & Safety – summary of any accidents, incidents, near misses, tool box talks, site meetings, HSE visits and contractors' internal H&S audits etc. This is always item 1 on the agenda of meetings and reports and sets the tone of priority across the development team.

- General summary of progress

- Programme - which shows their progress towards each of the milestones and tasks.

- Discharges – progress on approvals from statutory bodies such as building control, planning and structural warranty provider etc.

- RFI log - request for information log of any outstanding information or clarification the contractor is seeking (which could contain the potential for a variation event).

- Change control – variation register with any red, amber or green risks.

- Payments – schedule of monies due and paid ensuring close control on fiscal compliance.

- Photos – progress photos to track the visual progress of the project as well as identify any areas of concern.

- Handover documentation – monitor this from day 1 establishing milestones and formats so that it is constantly in the forefront of all party's mind.

- Neighbours – any issues with neighbour relations or complaints etc.

- Risk register

Risk management is key to any developer's repertoire. From the very earliest stages of your development opportunity there must be a development risk register. This should include all foreseeable risks and the more developments and the more accomplished you become, the more you will accumulate a 'standard' set of risks that are applied to any development as a useful checklist.

The typical areas will include the risk identification, ownership, risk rating, category, probability, impact and likely consequences.

You should assess the rating on a red, amber or green basis and then you will look at the mitigation measures. Once the mitigation measures have been undertaken, you will look at the probability impact and rating again. The net effect will be your residual risk and then you can quantify whether that residual risk is acceptable and how you will manage that residual risk through risk transfer to a party who is capable of managing that risk, or through specific other measures.

Risk management with your main contractor is important and you should place that obligation on your main contractor as well as yourself and your professional team, to uphold a project risk register where all parties are encouraged to contribute freely so they are 'forewarned is forearmed' with any approaching risks.

Typically the professional team monthly report will be undertaken by the lead designer, often the architect and will be tabled at the same meeting as the main contractor's report on a pre-scheduled monthly basis. The contents of the report will include:

- Health & Safety update
- Summary progress
- Design team obligations
- Main contractor progress
- Design progress update
- Change control
- Compliance – approvals, permissions and sign offs etc
- Quality
- Risks

Finally you will have an additional report when using an independent quantity surveyor outside of the design team, otherwise this would be incorporated within the design team report. This report would include detailed financial information including:

- Budget v actual
- Variation control register
- Anticipated final account
- Cash flow report
- Programme assessment
- Issues/concerns
- Risks

Change control

Change will happen on any development. It could be change of external circumstances, amendment to the specification, amendment to time or unforeseen circumstances on site being uncovered which need to be addressed, or many other scenarios.

As developers we need to have a robust change control process where each element is identified at the earliest possible stage, by the main contractor or professional team and reported appropriately for investigation to establish:

- What is the issue?
- Who is responsible?
- What are the mitigation measures?
- How will they be performed?
- What is the cause and effect on:
    - Design
    - Cost
    - Time

Each one of the potential cause and effects will need to be evaluated to ensure that the development economics are upheld and the final end product is not compromised.

Under contract during the construction period, delays and disruption must be recorded openly and on a very regular and immediate basis, between the developer, professional team and the main contractor. The delay must be identified irrespective of perceived cause. Any delay could be caused by developer, professional team, main contractors or an external party. The contract will prescribe who has the duty of care and where the cause and effect lies.

The contract administrator of the main contract will assess when an early warning is given, whether a variation event has occurred. That early warning must be raised as soon as it is reasonably apparent that a delay may, or is likely to occur. Once the identification of the relevant event has been made and that there is a likely delay, the contract administrator will investigate, ask for further and better particulars and may either:

- Accept the delay
- Grant an extension of time
- Grant additional costs
- May adjust the completion date accordingly for any hybrid of the above.

Any recovery or loss ensuing will be assessed to decide who will be responsible.

All parties have a responsibility to mitigate any delay and resulting loss that occurs. Solid communication and relations with your main contractor will help this, at all stages of the development. Assessing your contractor and your professional team with their potential to become part of your longer term professional team under the developments will pay strong dividends over time.

Disputes

Whilst far from ideal, disputes are part of life and they do occasionally happen. Assessing the claims of any extension of time, or early warning notices, must be undertaken quickly and swiftly.

Occasionally they can be complicated and controversy can exist. It is important that the main contractor and professional team value all variations quickly and effectively and try and agree each one in a timely manner, and not await their resolution at the end of the contract. Every effort should be used to resolve disputes prior to any formal dispute resolution being invoked.

Over several decades I have seen main contractor and professional team slug it out over variations and become entrenched in their own positions. Ultimately you as the client, the developer may have to take a pragmatic view and become involved before things escalate, emotions become charged and the overall development is impacted where it could otherwise have been resolved.

Calmness under pressure is a virtue and listening to your professional team and your main contractor may enable you to instruct a pragmatic decision to resolve for the overall good of the development. I have seen relatively small sums being so hotly contested that the resource required to debate and the delay in the development programme has far outweighed the cost of the variation.

Should a dispute not be able to be resolved, there are a number of paths to follow:

- Adjudication
- Arbitration
- Litigation

Alternative dispute resolution (ADR) is where a dispute can be placed in the hands of a third party adjudicator or arbitrator. This process is subject to strict timescales and will have a significant cost for your professional team to raise the correct documentation and supporting evidence for the adjudicator or arbitrator.

Litigation is another option. However, in many cases it is far from ideal to pursue any of these routes and solid resolute discussions and a fair approach with your main contractor generally will resolve most of your potential disputes, before they become major disputes requiring a third party intervention.

Handover

At the end of the construction phase, the developer will be required to accept the work from the main contractor. This will be done via your professional team, on your behalf, as it should commence at the beginning of the construction phase, not at the end!

All parties should be very aware of the obligations and responsibilities of what is required and when and this will be embedded in the contracts.

The main contractor will submit a notification for practical completion at a stage when they deem their work is complete. This of course should be of no surprise to you, as open communications and formal reporting will have been conducted in a very transparent manner, with anticipated dates being reported monthly.

There will be testing, commissioning, snagging and close out phases to your project, all programmed by your main contractor. All works should be snagged and closed out on a phase-by-phase basis to avoid a final issue towards the end of the project. However, miscellaneous elements will be picked up towards the end of the project.

Practical completion will be issued when all works are completed substantially, so be aware that this definition sometimes requires a little additional clarity for both parties to ensure no dispute occurs, particularly where variations have affected the course of the construction phase.

For every development to become complete requires a suite of documentation and this is required prior to the issuing of the certificate of practical completion.

All parties should be clear under the contract, of the information that is required in the handover documentation, which might include:

- Healthy and Safety file
- Building logbook
- Owner's manual
- As-built plans and information
- Notice of planning and discharges/compliance
- Building control records
- Test records and certificates

- Warranties
- Structural warranties
- Guarantees
- Appliance literature and user documents.

This can be an exhaustive supply of information and must be built up right from the start of the construction phase, rather than waiting towards the end.

On completion of the construction phase, a certificate of practical completion will be issued by the developer and the professional team to the main contractor.

Under most contracts, retention monies will have been held on the main contractor; typically somewhere between 3% to 5% of all application payments will have been retained.

"The entire contract administration process builds up towards your final account"

At practical completion, 50% of the retention money, i.e. 1.5% to 2.5%, would be released to the main contractor. At this point the defects liability period commences. Under most contracts, this would be 12 months; however, it can vary, subject to negotiation.

Any bonds or warranties that have been entered into potentially, may be released also at practical completion. The final account preparation should ideally be at an advanced level at this stage of the programme. The close out of the financial aspects of the contract to a successful and amicable conclusion, must be a priority.

The final account can take a substantial period of time and your contract administration during the development will have a significant bearing on the efficiency of agreement at the end of the contract. Therefore, the end result will be directly proportional to how accurately all variations, progress milestone updates and draw-down throughout the course of the project have been managed.

The entire contract administration process builds up towards your final account. Do not wait to draw the final account to a close solely at the end of the development.

Finally, during your post-completion phase, there will be a certificate of making good defects, which will be issued to the main contractor once you have inspected all the works at the end of the defects liability period. The defects liability period will be circa 12 months. At the end, this making good list will be offered to the main contractor, who will then undertake their own inspection, remedy any works, deal with any snags, defects and any contractual remaining obligations.

Latent defects are something you should be aware of as a developer as this covers defects generally through design, workmanship or materials. It would cover areas which are generally not apparent and detectable at practical completion. The limitations of the Latent Defects Act generally cover 12 years as a deed, or six years underhand and are an important part of your assurance process.

Any collateral warranties that have been entered into between developer, main contractor and the senior debt provider would generally be released at this point of time, at the end of the practical completion phase.

At the end of the 12 month making good defects period, once all obligations have been satisfied, the remaining 50% of retention monies, 1.5% - 2.5%, would be released to your main contractor.

Structural Warranties

With the sound advice always resonating in our mind of 'start with the end in mind' we must ensure that we walk a mile in our buyer's shoes, irrespective of whether our primary strategy is to sell the individual development units. Who knows what the future may hold or what any buying party's strategy may be down the line. A structural warranty is an insurance backed product which covers the structural integrity of the new home that has been created.

In a commercial-to-residential conversion or new-build development, we are by definition creating new residential units which will have a separate new title at land registry. The structural warranty will provide assurance to the funders and buyers of these new units, that they have been constructed to sound and recognised standards which have been independently verified.

The warranties that are provided within the industry are typically on a 10-year basis, however more lengthy periods are available.

The three key parties we must consider with regards to providing structural warranties are:

a. Development funder – the funder is fully focused on their clear route of exit and therefore insistent on ensuring the residential units that are developed are of solid credentials and ultimately fundable by future mortgage providers.

b. Buyer – the buyer's solicitor will be very familiar with new home warranties and will require a third party structural building warranty. Any concerns in this area may well cause delays or possibly put the sale at risk as each mortgage provider will be looking for assurance, prior to lending.

c. Help to Buy Scheme – This Government backed scheme has a small panel of mortgage providers and you, as a developer, will have no influence or control on which mortgage provider the buyer will use. The Help to Buy mortgage panel must comply with minimum requirements which include structural building warranties.

In our EquaGroup developments we have experienced mortgage providers for Help to Buy residential supported units not accepting a changing criterion on a large structural building warranty provider, rendering their cover as unacceptable to a large proportion of the market. If our monitoring and diligence had not flagged this movement in the market and thus potential risk midway through the construction phase, we would have had significant delays in the sale of the units towards the end of the development when funder due diligence would have identified the issues.

In this case, we had to switch warranty providers during the construction phase which, while problematic, we were able to resolve given that this was a permitted development refurbishment with little structural modifications to the existing building. However, imagine the challenges of switching warranty provider on a new-build or development where significant structural works had already been undertaken.

In order to provide the structural warranty, the following information is required:

- Regular audit checks at key stages of the development
- Building control certificate
- Planning permission evidenced as satisfied

When is the right time to start thinking of which warranty provider to use? Well, as early as possible and certainly well before any physical work starts on your development.

The recommendation would be to do your research into 3-4 warranty specialists during the later stages of the conveyancing phase of your development. Once you have achieved legal completion and are in the design phase, you can build all design, inspection and audit requirements into your designer and main contractors scope of works to ensure all parties are absolutely clear on the requirements and the importance of structural building warranties for your development - and indeed for the designer and main contractor under their contractual obligations!

At the end of the construction phase you must ensure that all obligations and pre-requisite conditions are satisfied to ensure that warranties are released and provided to the buyer's solicitor in good time to ensure no delay to the exchange and completion cycle of the sale of the apartments or houses.

Care in this area will result in a swift and expedient exit from your development and thus almost certainly resulting in much reduced cost of funds from your senior debt provider and a greater ROCE for your investors as a result of reduced costs and time of the development.

Home User Guide

The aim of the Home User Guide is to help give residents an introduction to their new home and surrounding areas.

The guide itself has explanations of the equipment features installed, how to use them effectively and maintenance instructions to ensure that your home functions as efficiently as possible. It also provides tips on how to live a more sustainable life resulting in savings on energy, water and household running costs.

It gives details of the local waste collection services, such as the day of the week for collection.

It gives the address and contact numbers for your local GP, Chemist, transport, other local amenities and emergency information.

The home user guide contains links to useful information and services within your homes area.

A typical content list might consider contents such as:

- Introduction
- Heating & Cooling
- Window Operation & Care
- Doors
- Kitchen
- Sanitaryware
- Engineered Wood Flooring
- Gas and Water Points
- Electrical
- Smoke Detectors & Fire Alarm
- Appliance Instructions and Warranty Details
- Sustainable DIY
- Water Use
- Recycling & Waste Collections
- Public Transport
- Local Amenities
- Emergency Information
- Fire Safety
- Defects
- Certificates

- Appendices
- Health & Safety File

Modular Construction

Trends in modern construction methods are moving rapidly with increased drives towards:

- Increasing quality
- Reducing time to market
- Reducing waste and environmental footprint
- Improved predictability
- Reducing costs of construction
- Reducing overall costs

I first came across and deployed 400,000m2+ of modular construction units across two global infrastructure rollouts in the 1990s.

1. Mobile base station infrastructure where our telecommunications hubs were factory manufactured to high tolerances, quality control levels and craned on to site from the back of a lorry. Installation time was about one hour, with only power connection, fixing down bolts and bonding and earthing required before the final antenna and feeder cabling could be concluded.

2. Data Centres where vast warehouses often 30,000m2+ each, were converted into the highest levels of globally resilient Tier data centres supporting some of the largest trading gateways in the world. Structural Insulated Panels (SIP) were extensively utilised during their construction.

Time is the most expensive commodity within developments as a rule. The uncertainty that design and then build/refurbishment programmes can take, all requires substantial funding lines of senior debt, bridge, mezzanine and private capital to varying degrees.

To reduce the development timelines to create a factory-engineered and manufactured quality of build, in dry conditions, with minimal site preparation above ground, can save substantial amounts of funding costs and with a transformation of gross profit levels, could well determine an entirely different and more rewarding funding structure.

Some of the benefits that modular construction can deliver to a development include:

- Factory levels of quality
- Weather independent
- Reduced design input as designs become modular
- No wet trades or drying out required
- More controlled factory environment with reduced Health and Safety risks
- Speed of erection on site
- Documentation and certification available immediately prior to delivery
- Reduce site congestion and logistics
- Reduced wastage
- Improved environmental credentials
- Costs more predictable
- Reduced funding costs
- Reduced monitoring surveyor fees due to reduce construction phase.

To balance the benefits, the developer embracing this rapidly emerging construction method should also be mindful to ensure the following areas are formalised and verified successfully before commencing to avoid issues later down the line:

- Securing development finance
- Funder approval for modular construction method
- Funder approval of modular manufacturer
- Structural warranty provision
- Insurability during construction
- Acceptability to target market
  - Re-finance to hold

- Private sales market
- Private Rental Sector (PRS)

- Compatibility with Help To Buy Scheme and their approved mortgage providers
- Appetite of buyers

Pause for thought - Negotiating with Congruency

My first mentor back in 1992 mentioned the quote "Walk a mile in another person's shoes" and it has stuck with me, defined me and served me well in high-level corporate negotiations, business transactions, M&A, contract discussions, property deals and securing mutually agreeable terms, time and time again.

It has also served me well in problem solving, which is a fundamental pillar of what I have always done. If you can understand where someone else is in life, what their circumstances are, what they consider as a great series of outcomes and crucially, cement a bond of trust that enables transparency, you are far better able to position a win:win outcome.

Our business is EquaGroup and the EQUA stands for our values of Creating Shared Value.

If you can inspire deal creation and problem solving and work in an equitable manner where all parties come out of the final deal with what they expected, then you will be able to create an extremely stable and sustainable business founded on solid bedrock. In our day-to-day businesses, we regularly assess our societal partners and what great looks like to them and of our many 'partners in success' - how many of your stakeholders do you consider a 'partner in your success'? It is extremely thought-provoking and I strongly recommend you do this with each transaction.

Your values define YOU and your modus operandi, they are not skin deep - they form part of your DNA.

Negotiating is hard and you must be firm, know your position and be clear. However, this can be done professionally in any circumstances - "It is not just what you do, it is how you do it". So remember or when making offers, negotiating, examining how to do a deal, working with private investors etc, always start with open questions to understand who would be invested in the deal, what each party's circumstances are, what an acceptable outcome would look like and when and how that can be accomplished to the satisfaction of all parties.

Seasoned negotiating starts with who you are, how you ask open questions and absolutely how you then listen. People might remember what you said or when you said it - they will definitely remember how you made them feel. I wish you well as you create shared value in everything you do for you and your 'partners'.

12. Exit

I'm a very positive thinker, and I think that is what helps me the most in difficult moments —
Roger Federer

Start with the end in mind. Sound advice that we know should be heeded as a developer of commercial conversions. The starting point as we look at any potential deal or assess our area, should be to understand what our exit strategy or strategies are. Always prepare at least two exit strategies, but ensure you are comfortable with your core strategy.

"Always prepare at least two exit strategies"

There are a number of dependencies in your business operations and how you select your exit strategy might be based in part on:

- Business structure
- Tax strategy
- Type and volume of your target market
- Expertise
- How you fund
- Aspirations of your JV partners and their exit strategy

What could your exit options look like? Typically, they fall into a number of categories. You could:

- Buy, develop, title split and sell
- Buy, develop and sell a non-title split block
- Buy, develop and hold
- Combination of buy developed and partially hold and sell some units
- Buy, add value and sell before developing
- Buy, add value and sell, retaining some equity
- Contract and develop would typically be working with alternative funding, typically 100% loan to cost structures

Each one of these strategies will have a very specific set of criteria and considerations. These will vary and be not limited to the following:

- How you fund your development
- How you purchase your development
- Company structure

- Resources you have available
- Expertise you have available
- Phase two funding

Selling strategy

Your sales strategy will need to commence at the very earliest time of completing on the acquisition of the property. From this point on every step taken is about aligning the right product to the right market and at the right time, to optimise your return in as short a period of time as possible.

Factors you will need to be aware of include:

- Timing with the economic cycle of the development duration
- Timing within the year - launching the various stages of your marketing as Christmas, Easter and summer will bring different challenges and indeed opportunities.
- Early sales and optimising timescales v longer duration whilst maximising sales value
- Cost of funding your development

Note that some forms of development finance will only allow phased drawdowns, subject to off-plan sales performance, to release the next phase funding tranche. However, this is usually applicable to much larger developments.

Predominantly, there are four sales strategies which we covered in the marketing section earlier. They are:

1. Very early - off plan pre-development commencement
2. Early – off plan post development commencement
3. Completed show apartment
4. Late sale of actual apartment

Technology is starting to change the way we market property and inevitably this will create a shift in society where virtualisation, augmented reality and virtual reality become the expected norm. We are seeing some fantastic software emerging which will help viewers purchase of property through virtual walk-through of the finished product whilst the development has yet to commence. Through computer-generated graphics packages and the use of our smartphones, location becomes less relevant when identifying new home purchase.

It is true to say this is still an emerging market and it is yet to be seen how early adopters and customers adapt to this and whether it will replace the actual visit and brochures, I think we can see that the trend is increasing all the time and we should see some very significant and exciting change in this marketplace in the future.

Engaging investors, whether they be long-term pension funds or individual personal investors, is another strategy for sale on masse for non-title split developments. This can be pre-agreed prior, during or at completion of the development, depending on the risk appetite of the investment party. Not all investors would be looking at a discount to market in their purchase as they may have other considerations ranging from tax efficiency, alternative strategy to increase value or long range investment horizons.

Help to Buy

Given the significant shortage of homes nationwide, the Government has introduced incentive schemes to stimulate the market for developers to build new homes and for buyers to buy.

Help To Buy Scheme is the most well-known and was introduced by the Home and Communities Agency in 2014 and is designed to enable further home ownership to be accessible to more people.

This scheme does not necessarily impact the developer directly although indirectly, it most certainly does form a significant advantage in the sales process.

Help To Buy can enable first time buyers to buy with a very low deposit, possibly even as little as 5% of purchase price.

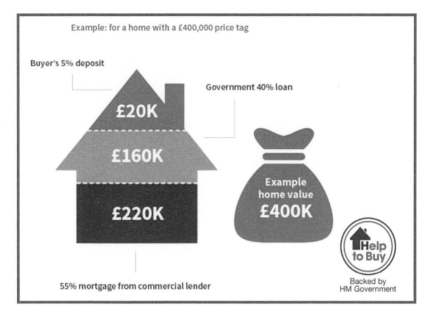

The following is a summary of the process used to apply for Help to Buy. Note that this process can only be initiated when you possess 'significant control' of the site. Typically, a developer would start the process of applying for Help To Buy after exchange of contracts.

The link below will take you to the registering website:
https://ims.homesengland.org.uk/Register/HelpToBuy

1. Complete the account registration for the Development SPV
2. Activate your Homes and Communities Agency (HCA) account
3. To begin, click 'Submit Forecast' and select the financial year your development will complete.
4. Enter the following details in the editable boxes:
   - Local Authority
   - Number of sites (generally one)
   - Legal completions (number of units to be created)
   - Equity Loan funding

5. HCA will send you a draft Help to Buy Contract that will outline your initial allowance of funding.
6. Send HCA the details of two people - either two directors or one director and one secretary - to enter and sign the Help to Buy contracts.
7. HCA send final contracts for signature
8. Conclude the Condition Precedent letters with your solicitor.
9. HCA confirm your allocated funding.

At a recent development, Oak House, our development company, EquaGroup secured confirmation of 7 out of 16 apartments for Help To Buy support.

Following the careful launch of phase one of the sales, we secured all 7 sales reservations within hours of the launch. A 100% phase reservation confirmation!

We contacted the Help To Buy scheme and advised them of the clear demand in the area and the response to phase one sales release. They suggested we resubmit our application for the remaining 9 apartments.

After only a few weeks, they responded and duly granted approval for Help To Buy on the remaining 9 apartments, thus giving 100% coverage across the entire development.

Persistence - the time honoured quote of 'if at first you don't succeed, try, try and try again' springs to mind!

Title Splitting - Freehold and Leasehold

Whether the strategy is buy, develop, sell or buy, develop and hold, the developer must understand how the freehold and leasehold system operates to evaluate the correct strategy to deploy, to meet their goals.

Typically, when approaching a title split strategy, the freehold of the property would be split into a number of leaseholds. Each lease would be between:

*   99 years

- 125 years
- 999 years

Most apartments are sold on a leasehold basis and typically 125 years would be very common.

The 999-year lease is often referred to as virtual freehold and while on the face of it, appears advantageous, be aware that the obligations and permissions are where the perils may lie in the future.

For example, imagine a development where you own an office, held on a 999-year lease that sits above a retail unit on a High Street location.

If you wished to develop the upper office floor levels, you would be required to contact the freeholder on the following elements:

- Approval from the freeholder for changes
- Responsibility for the freeholder's professional fees to consider your application/request.
- Bound by the timescales it takes the freeholder to negotiate and communicate.
- Pay a fee to freeholder to develop
- Pay all freeholder costs

Many freehold investments are held by large pension companies and quite possibly by offshore legal entities or investors based abroad – so beware of the bureaucracy and timescales that these negotiations can entail if you are considering purchasing and developing a virtual freehold commercial or residential property. It may be wise to add freeholder approval to the conditionality of your offer.

There are a number of key components to freeholds which must be appreciated and four of the most relevant are:

1. Ground rent
2. Service charge
3. Terms of the lease
4. Enhanced value potential

"add freeholder approval to the conditionality of your offer"

Ground Rents

Freehold buyers are parties who the developer will be looking to sell the freehold interests to and who in turn, will be looking at value extraction in a number of potential areas including annual ground rents over a long period of time, between 125 – 999 years.

For further details we will go into more depth in the following chapter on Terms of the Lease.

Service Charges

Management company and service charge fees will be established within the leasehold documentation. This has strong governance attached to it and is a specialist area.

Consideration may be given towards wider picture economies of scale on the service provision of the freehold provider and the management company. This may include services such as administration, insurance, gardening, window cleaning, overhead efficiency and rebates etc.

Terms of Lease

The terms of the lease may offer additional potential for the freeholder with areas such as long-term escalations and indexation. This is a core area that lobby groups and government are focusing in on, at the time of writing, and this will come under increased scrutiny.

Indexation on leasehold agreements may be in a number of different formats with the primary methods of tracking indexation being influenced and contracted by:

- Retail Price Index (RPI)
- Consumer Price Index (CPI)

- Bank of England Inflation Rate

However, the issue has been prevailing over the past few decades where seemingly innocuous provisions have made their way into leases which may contract an entirely different indexation structure.

For example, a 125-year lease had a ground rent provision of £250 per annum.

If this is not paid annually by the leaseholder then action would be taken by the freeholder which, ultimately could result in the leaseholder losing their property. This is highly unlikely to happen for the sake of £250 p.a.

This is why the covenant strength of this type of investment is considered exceptional and the yield will possibly be 3% – 5%.

If the indexation is at 3% p.a. for example, then the £250 would rise to circa £614.21 in 30 years' time.

However, what if a provision had been made in the lease that ground rents would double every five years? Seems pretty minor on the face of it and that is exactly what many thought no doubt when entering into these contracts. However, £250 doubled every five years would mean a ground rent in 30 years' time of £16,000!

An apartment with a ground rent escalation of this level would render the apartment unlikely to be sold and if it is unlikely to be sold, the owners are unlikely to also get a mortgage on the property. A huge issue for the leaseholder.

This would create a massive dilemma and this is what is unfolding across the country as a result of 'unfair' contracts that parties have entered into many years ago.

Enhanced Value Potential

This will include extracting additional value out of property through a use of:

- Air space – additional floors
- Loft conversion
- Basement conversion

- Further land development in gardens/car parks
- Efficiency of future expenses
- Long-term relaxation of the planning system enabling further upside

The example earlier in the chapter about the conversion of the offices above a retail unit on a virtual lease, brings the Freeholder 'enhanced value' element into sharp contrast.

When considering title splitting your freehold into individual leaseholds, it is important to understand the key implications of the lease and its specific terms. As developers, we are trying to strike a balance here between favourable terms which will add value to the freehold sale. We're also looking at terms which are attractive and fair to our purchases of the leasehold parties.

Government is increasingly taking measures in evaluating the fairness of leaseholds. We can expect in the next few years a tightening of the governance around the creation of leaseholds in apartments and new build and again, this is a very specialist area where specialist advice must be sought.

We have to strike a balance between creating great value for our freeholder and great security in value for our leasehold purchase, so that:

- Our lenders will be able to fund the purchase.
- The buyers will be able to buy.
- The freeholders will see value and will acquire the freehold.

This represents a win-win-win for the three parties - the buyers of the individual units and the freehold and ourselves as the developer.

SECTION THREE

CONCLUSION

He who has a why to live for can bear almost any how - Viktor Frankl

Final thoughts

I have been involved in converting commercial property in a variety of sizes, shapes and forms for more than 20 years.

What was incredibly important to me in writing this book was to stay true to my values. I am a risk manager at heart who understands the business of taking measured risk to liberate opportunity.

I was very clear from the outset that this book would reveal the REALITY of what it takes to operate commercial property conversion and development properly and with 'eyes wide open'.

For my clients attending my course or for those I mentor, I always finish with the following question "So what will you do at 8 o'clock tomorrow morning?"

Well what will YOU do?

I am someone who has a sense of purpose and urgency in everything I do - that also includes having fun by the way!

You have made an investment in purchasing this book which I thank you for – more importantly you have invested quite a few hours in reading the book.

The next vital step for you is starting your journey by considering each step in this book in the order it has been written to provide you with a roadmap to frame your engagement and resource allocation into defining with clarity, your next steps to success in the conversion and development of commercial property.

When stepping up to larger property developments such as commercial conversions and land developments, a number of things increase substantially:

- Size of the prize!
- The potential risk
- Ability to manage the risk
- Creation of Shared Value
- Ability to leverage experience
- Quantum of resources available to you
- Scale

- Timescales

I wish you the very best in succeeding in your objectives as you continue your evolution in this detailed yet exceptionally rewarding strategy.

Mark Stokes

Do or do not, there is no try - Yoda

Want to find out more?

If you think education is expensive, try ignorance

I have mentored people since the mid 1990's and also been a non-executive director since 2009. I hope I have been able to convey the wisdom that others have imparted in me and my years of experience, across to you.

If you have been inspired by this book, my story and the detail of operating a development business with a high performance culture and systems, then please contact me through social media for more details about the following:

- Advanced Commercial Developers' Course
- Bespoke 1-2-1 mentorship

If you would like to follow me and our businesses, I can be found on social media here:

Instagram   markstokes.stokes

Facebook   markstokes.stokes

LinkedIn   mark-stokes

Twitter   @markelstead

Email: mark.stokes@equagroup.co.uk

www.equagroup.co.uk

www.markstokesuk.com

IF – Rudyard Kipling

IF you can keep your head when all about you
Are losing theirs and blaming it on you,
If you can trust yourself when all men doubt you,
But make allowance for their doubting too;
If you can wait and not be tired by waiting,
Or being lied about, don't deal in lies,
Or being hated, don't give way to hating,
And yet don't look too good, nor talk too wise:
If you can dream - and not make dreams your master;
If you can think - and not make thoughts your aim;
If you can meet with Triumph and Disaster
And treat those two impostors just the same;
If you can bear to hear the truth you've spoken
Twisted by knaves to make a trap for fools,
Or watch the things you gave your life to, broken,
And stoop and build 'em up with worn-out tools:
If you can make one heap of all your winnings
And risk it on one turn of pitch-and-toss,
And lose, and start again at your beginnings
And never breathe a word about your loss;
If you can force your heart and nerve and sinew
To serve your turn long after they are gone,
And so hold on when there is nothing in you
Except the Will which says to them: 'Hold on!'
If you can talk with crowds and keep your virtue,
' Or walk with Kings - nor lose the common touch,
If neither foes nor loving friends can hurt you,
If all men count with you, but none too much;
If you can fill the unforgiving minute
With sixty seconds' worth of distance run,
Yours is the Earth and everything that's in it,
And - which is more - you'll be a Man, my son!

Making a Difference through Creating Shared Value

Being good is good business - Anita Roddick

This book will be an incubator for making a difference in society in more ways than one. As well as the huge societal benefits that this property strategy delivers, this book will further enable many future generations to create a compounding force for good as the benefits radiate through society.

My personal value system and that of our Equa business and culture, is based upon a passion and belief in Creating Shared Value in society.

An important function of this book, as well as sharing knowledge to our readers, is to distribute a proportion of the funds to worthy causes and create a positive impact in the world.

One option was to donate to a worthy charity, of which I studied many extremely worthy and humbling causes.

A quote which embodies my beliefs sprang to mind during my reflections:

"give a man a fish and you feed him for a day; teach a man to fish and you feed him for a lifetime"

I was clear that a proportion of the proceeds of this book should not just be donated in a single act to a great cause but should be delivered into a system which recycles the benefit time and time again, becoming an evergreen agent for positive change in the communities it serves.

These proceeds should also celebrate, embrace and symbolise the global momentum towards entrepreneurship and support those prepared to take a risk, seize an opportunity to create their own personal economy, which will in turn, create shared value in their local communities.

The funds are not donated in the traditional manner and are in fact loaned at a 0% interest rate and returned after a prescribed period of time, enabling funds to be reinvested time and time and time again, helping huge numbers of people many times over compared to what a single traditional donation might support.

After much deliberation I decided to support a variety of entrepreneurs throughout the world through microfinance, in particular through the terrific work undertaken by Lendwithcare.

For more information about the great work that Lendwithcare do, check out their website: www.lendwithcare.org

lendwithcare.org
Microloans from CARE International UK

Make a loan, change a life

care

lendwithcare

SECTION FOUR

APPENDICES

Invest in as much of yourself as you can, you are your own biggest asset by far - Warren Buffett

Demystifying Calculations

Calculations – demystified and made easy. Whilst this book is not about becoming an expert in accounting, it is important for us to understand the fundamentals of investment of our valuable resources such as economic capital and our own time.

GP: Gross Profit

Gross Profit is the difference between revenue and the cost of producing the product or service BEFORE deducting overhead, interest costs and tax etc.

NP: Net Profit

Net Profit is the difference between revenue and the cost of producing the product or service AFTER deducting overhead, interest costs and tax etc

ROI: Return on Investment

ROI is used to evaluate company investments using their cash flow and is shown as a percentage calculated as follows:

Return on Investment = (Profit from Investment – Cost of Investment)/Cost of Investment

ROCE: Return on Capital Employed

ROCE measures how efficiently a business uses the capital it has. Property represents a different position for many investors as a substantial proportion of the capital required for the purchase and development may have come from commercial lenders. Hence it is important to understand the returns on the proportion of the capital the investor has invested. The following calculation will provide this

Return on Capital Employed = Earnings before interest and tax (EBIT)/Capital Employed

ROTE: Return on Time Employed

Given that our time is the scarcest resource we have, it would make sense to measure the return on each hour/day/week we spend on any given opportunity which can then aid us in measuring existing ROTE and selecting future opportunity potential, sometimes referred to a Return on time Employed (ROTI). The calculation can be made in terms of revenue or sales, however as entrepreneurs it is more commonly used in terms of net profits.

Return on Time Employed = Total Net profit/Time invested

NPV: Net Present Value

The value of money today, compared to the future value it will have when it has been invested at compound interest.

£1,100 due in 12 months' time has a present value of £1,000 today, if invested at an annual rate of 10%

IRR: Internal Rate of Return

The internal rate of return on an investment or project is the "annualised effective compounded return rate" or "rate of return" that sets the net present value of all cash flows (both positive and negative) from the investment equal to zero.

DCF: Discounted Cash Flow

Discounted cash flow is a method of analysing the value of a project, company, or asset using the concepts of the time value of money. All future cash flows are estimated and discounted by using cost of capital to give their present values.

Yield

Gross Yield is the income return on an investment before expenses are deducted

Gross Yield = Annual Income/Property Value

Net Yield is the income return on an investment after all costs have been deducted. These costs can include, but not be limited to the following:

- Commercial funding costs
- Business rates
- Management fees
- Insurance

- Repairs and maintenance
- Acquisition costs
- Security

Net Yield = (Annual Income – All costs)/Property Value

Property Value using Rental Income

A commercial property is often valued based on its annual income as follows:

- Property Value = (Annual Rental Income / Yield) x 100
- Annual Rental Income = £210,000
- Yield = 7%
- Property Value:
- Property Value = (£210,000 / 7) x 100
- Property Value = £3 Million

Glossary of Terms

PDR	Permitted Development Rights
NIA	Net Internal Area
GIA	Gross Interior Area
GEA	Gross External Area
GDV	Gross Development Value
SPV	Special Purpose Vehicle
LLP	Limited Liability Partnership
JCT	Joint Contracts Tribunal
NEC	New Engineering Contract
D&B	Design & Build
CDM	Construction Design Management: 2015 Regulations
CPD	Continuous Professional Development
CSV	Creating Shared Value
ROI	Return on Investment
ROCE	Return on Capital Employed
ROTE	Return on Time Employed
SIPP	Self Invested Personal Pension
SSAS	Small Self-Administered Pension Scheme
NEC	New Engineering Contract: Standard form of Contract
RICS	Royal Institution of Chartered Surveyors: Professional body
CIOB	Chartered Institute of Building
CIBSE	Chartered Institution of Building Services Engineers
RIBA	Royal Institute of British Architects
ISE	The Institution of Structural Engineers
EPC	Energy Performance Certificate
CPSE	Commercial Property Standard Enquiries
PV	Photovoltaic (solar) panel
ITT	Invitation to tender

SAP	Standard Assessment Procedure
PEA	Predicted Energy Assessment
VC	Venture Capital
JV	Joint Venture
HSE	Health & Safety Executive
COSHH	Control of Substances Hazardous to Health
AIB	Asbestos Insulating Board
RIDDOR	Reporting of Injuries, Diseases and Dangerous Occurrences Regulations
DSE	Display Screen Equipment
PAT	Portable Appliance Testing
LOI	Letter of Intent
KPI	Key Performance Indicator
KBI	Key Business Indicator
HCA	Homes and Communities Agency
HoT's	Heads of Terms
SDLT	Stamp Duty Land Tax
CAs	Capital Allowances
MEES	Minimum Energy Efficiency Standards
VOA	Valuation Office Agency
HMRC	HM Revenue & Customs
CIL	Community Infrastructure Levy
AH	Affordable Homes
HTB	Help to Buy
S106	Section 106
VBC	Vacant Building Credit
IPMS	International Property Management Standards
ILA	Independent Legal Advice
TOGC	Transfer of Going Concern
BAFO	Best and final offer

ESG   Enviromental, social and goverance
AIB   Asbestos Insulating Board
LDC   Lawful Development Certificate
ADR   Alternative Despite Resolution

Useful Links

EquaGroup

www.equagroup.co.uk

Synergy Funding

www.synergyfunding.co.uk

Technical housing standards – nationally described space standard
- https://assets.publishing.service.gov.uk/government/uploads/
system/uploads/attachment_data/file/524531/160519_
Nationally_Described_Space_Standard____Final_Web_version.pdf

Health & Safety Executive

http://www.hse.gov.uk

Land Registry

https://www.gov.uk/government/organisations/land-registry

RICS

https://www.rics.org/uk/

RICS Property Measurement

http://www.rics.org/Global/prop%20
measurement_2ndedition_2018.pdf

Financial Conduct Authority

https://www.fca.org.uk

FCA 13/3 Guidance
https://www.fca.org.uk/publication/policy/ps13-03.pdf

Government Planning
www.gov.uk/guidance/local-plans

Experian
http://experian.co.uk

Energy Performance Certificate
http://epcregister.com

Help To Buy
https://www.helptobuy.gov.uk

Help To Buy (Register)
https://ims.homesengland.org.uk/Register/HelpToBuy

Ministry of Housing Communities and Local Government -
https://www.gov.uk/government/organisations/ministry-of-
housing-communities-and-local-government

Minimum Energy Efficiency standards
http://www.rics.org/uk/knowledge/glossary/minimum-energy-
efficiency-standard-/

Building Regulations
https://www.gov.uk/building-regulations-approval

Estates Gazette
https://www.egi.co.uk

Daltons Business
https://www.daltonsbusiness.com

Fleurets
https://www.fleurets.com

Christie & Co
https://www.christie.com

Stamp Duty Land Tax
https://www.gov.uk/stamp-duty-land-tax

The Town & Country Planning (General Permitted Development) Order 2016
http://www.legislation.gov.uk/uksi/2016/332/pdfs/uksi_20160332_en.pdf

Property Week
https://www.propertyweek.com

Land InSight

https://www.landinsight.io

Rightmove

http://www.rightmove.co.uk

Zoopla

https://www.zoopla.co.uk

Primelocation

https://www.primelocation.com

Valuation Office Agency

https://www.gov.uk/government/organisations/valuation-office-agency

Proof of Address

https://www.royalmail.com/find-a-postcode

Credit Report (Company + Individual)

https://www.experian.co.uk/consumer/index-496.html

Companies House -

https://beta.companieshouse.gov.uk/

Company & Director Check too all current & dissolved companies
https://companycheck.co.uk/

Land Registry
https://eservices.landregistry.gov.uk/.../04.../

Bankruptcy Search
https://www.gov.uk/search-bankruptcy-insolvency-register

London Gazette
https://www.thegazette.co.uk/

Community Infrastructure Levy
https://www.gov.uk/guidance/community-infrastructure-levy#charging-schedule-overarch-section

World forum on National Capital
https://naturalcapitalfourm.com